Rhythms of Resilience is a godsend in this period of history. I pastor people who have experienced trauma, depression, poverty, and abuse. Because I live and work in a third-world country, I also experience chaos. Phil's book reminds us that the joy of the Lord is our strength. The faith practices he writes about are exactly what I have needed in this difficult and chaotic season of life. I highly recommend this book to anyone who feels overwhelmed and burdened.

Let the Spirit minister to you through this book and walk away with practical tools to be more encouraged, resilient, and at peace.

—Rev. Roger Lam
Pastor, Missionary, and Social Entrepreneur

As a Christian mental health therapist, I cannot thank Phillip Chan enough for writing this book, especially when we need it most. I highly recommend this book to anyone who recognizes God's calling in their lives. It will help you grow and flourish in a world where you may feel you are barely staying afloat.

Rhythms of Resilience welcomes us into a deeper sense of self through a return to our spiritual senses, abidance in Christ, and offering us the opportunity to prosper instead of survive. Phillip Chan guides the reader towards being intentional in these essential steps of realigning our hearts and minds back to the source of our strength and then bringing that strength into the chaos surrounding us. If you feel lost in the chaos, and want vital and practical tools to reclaim your spiritual and mental/emotional wholeness, then this book is a must-read for you.

I am excited for you, reader, to reclaim a life worth living and to walk on the waters with Him in the midst of the storm.

—Daniel Wongthavatchai, LCSW
Mental Health Therapist

Rhythms of Resilience is a practical guide for living intentionally and on purpose—not just when life is easy but especially when life is chaotic. If you have been experiencing conflict in your relationships or have been feeling anxious, depressed, or stuck, not knowing what to do next in life, this book is for you. No matter your Christian faith tradition, all can adopt these practices. They will be particularly beneficial for those whose Christian experience has not emphasized contemplative practice as a way of life.

The practices Phil describes in easy-to-follow steps encompass the totality of the human experience. I especially appreciate Phil's transparency and authenticity in conveying his actual daily struggles. His authenticity allows the reader to lower their shame shields to be genuine in their practice of the rhythms as well.

As a culture, we have become accustomed to numbing ourselves from our pain rather than digging in to grow and become more fully who God has called us to be. Phil intended this psychologically-minded practical guide for people who desire to grow and are unsatisfied with the status quo. If you adopt even some of these practices, undoubtedly, your life will be transformed.

—Rachel Keener, PsyD
Licensed Clinical Psychologist

Having spent the last several years serving and counseling missionaries overseas, I see how crucial Phil's *Rhythms of Resilience* is to staying grounded in Jesus during the inevitable storms that come in our lifetimes. Phil reminds us that it isn't perfection that Jesus wants from us. He desires a willingness to step into practical ways to connect us to the Father when everything is going sideways.

—Carol K.

Missions Director and Former Missionary

Rhythms of Resilience is an invaluable resource that highlights a path to developing spiritual strength to flourish in difficult times. This hands-on guide will allow you to develop routines and practices to take back a sense of empowerment and control. This book offers real and approachable tools that challenge many of today's stress-provoking routines. It provides real-life examples of engaging one's spiritual well-being to move from feeling overwhelmed and powerless to a place of deeper connection and inner rest.

—Kristi Wollbrink

Associate Marriage and Family Therapist

The timeliness of this book is striking to me. Looking back, the cascading waves of personal, emotional, relational, political, financial, and (inter)-national chaos we've all tried to endure this decade are dramatic. And with this realization comes the sense that chaos is the new normal. As Christians, we must remember that if God knows all things, then this period of tumult—as well as what is to come—is not unknown by God.

Surviving and being a leader in chaos requires us not to respond to it from chaos in our hearts but from peace and rest. The extremity of our chaotic world takes men and women who will make space for God's peace to rest deep within them. That's the kingdom of heaven that's supposed to come through us, after all.

For this reason, I'm grateful for Phil and what he's written. The four rhythms and the associated practices help us to create habits of looking reflectively at the game tapes of our lives. With always-on shouting of twenty-four-hour news and noisy social media, we must intentionally create space to hear God's still, small voice within us. This book is the place to start.

With Holy Spirit as our coach, God's intention is to strengthen and build us up for the days ahead. Let's dive in and let God prepare us for the world He knows is coming.

—Rev. John Lo, DMin
Senior Pastor, Epicentre Church Pasadena

FAITH PRACTICES *to*
THRIVE *in* CHAOS

Rhythms of Resilience

PHIL CHAN

BERRY
POWELL
PRESS

First paperback edition December 2022
Cover Design by Kimberly Tsui Fong
Interior Design by Formatted Books
Published by Berry Powell Press
Glendora, California
www.berrypowellpress.com

ISBN: 978-1-957321-10-3 (Paperback)
ISBN: 978-1-957321-11-0 (ebook)
Library of Congress Control Number: 2022922174

Contents

To Esther:
I am honored to hold hands with you at our world's end.
You are the rock of our family.

To Vera, Jubilee, Nova, and Titan:
Your presence is a gift from God to me.
I hope that when I grow up, I shall be like you.

Acknowledgments

Of all the people I owe thanks to, the first and foremost is my wife. Esther—what can I say? Without you, this book would literally be impossible. You have been my number-one cheerleader and challenger. You have made many sacrifices to see this through, from watching the kids so I can write to processing the ups and downs of all my emotions. Though it was my hands at the keyboard, your fingerprints run through this book as well. I hope you will see many blessed by the support you gave to this work.

Vera, Jubilee, Nova, and Titan, thank you for supporting daddy as he spent many hours writing. Your constant knocking on my door to show me pictures, play games, and get my attention were no interruptions. They were a reminder of why what I wrote was important. It's so other people and I can be the best at being faithful to the important things. Thank you for the joy you brought me throughout the writing of this book.

Carmen, I am glad I remind you of yourself. I know that must have contributed to your great patience with me these two years. Thank you for graciously giving me a chance to write, coaching me through it, and publishing my very first book. Your impact on my life will never be forgotten.

Abby, thank you for your tireless hours coaching, encouraging, and editing. I am always strengthened by your challenges and encouragement throughout this long process. Thank you, especially for the last phase of editing. Your words in the book made it truly come to life in ways I never could.

Mom, Dad, Eunice, Diane, and Ruth, thanks for being such a warm and supportive presence toward me my whole life, including all the ups and downs my faith journey has taken me on. Each of you has shaped me in ways that have culminated in this book.

John Lo, thank you for pastoring me all these years. Not only are you quoted numerous times in this book, but your wisdom and guidance permeate nearly every page. Your love for Esther and me has made this possible.

Jude Tiersma Watson, thank you for teaching and guiding me in one of my last classes at Fuller. I usually sat in the back, listening and half paying attention, but let this be an encouragement that the seeds you plant go further than you see. Thank you for introducing me to contemplative practices. I hope another generation will see their wisdom and efficacy for the lives we lead.

Janice, thanks for encouraging me in our time leading life group together. Thanks also for spending an evening hashing out ideas for the book. Rest assured, the concepts you helped me refine made it!

Mike and Judy, thanks for being close companions through the trials of the last few years. Your friendship was a source of warmth in a cold world.

Eric Chang, I heard you put me in your acknowledgments in your book. So here I am returning the favor.

Kim, thank you for being a great friend since our youth. It is amazing to see our lives intertwine yet again for God's work. Thank you for lending your creative and artistic mind to see this book reach the hands of someone who would not have otherwise noticed it.

Dan, thank you for your constant encouragement. Thank you for listening to my crazy ideas and encouraging me that the insights God gave me were worth sharing.

Fiona, thank you for all your wisdom and for introducing me to Dallas Willard, whose words are woven into this book.

Thank you to the rest of the Berry Powell Press team, including Valeri Mills Barnes, Carolyn Rafferty, Marianne Croonquist, and Kathleen Taylor. Each of you played an essential role in this book's growth process and fruition.

Introduction

Looking back to my days shortly after college, I recall that the doomsday cycle on the news was never-ending. I felt continually confronted with national or international crisis after crisis. Just when I started to recover from the last crisis, another one was just around the corner. Anxiety and a sense of helplessness were daily emotions.

In addition, there were stresses in my life—with my schooling, my wife and family, my career, and simple daily living. When I looked around, I saw many people were having trouble managing the complexities of life. Like a swirling wind that increases in size and speed, the collective anxiety was distressing and crippling.

I didn't know how to deal with this, but I realized something was missing in my Christian walk if checking social media could knock me off balance.

It wasn't until I took a Fuller Seminary class that I was able to identify this missing element. I'd been a Christian for many years, having grown up evangelical and later moved in a charismatic direction. Taught by Professor Jude Tiersma Watson, the class exposed me to a wide range of spiritual practices that spanned across time, nationality, and denominations—especially within Catholic, Orthodox, and Protestant traditions. Many core practices were familiar to me. Still, I discovered new emphases and ways of living them out. I was fascinated by them, and they challenged the limited paradigm I'd developed around spiritual practices that ground our faith.

While the intellectual knowledge was new and interesting to me, the true impact of the course was from one of the professor's homework assignments. This practice was rooted in the monastic tradition, initially led by a group of third-century men named the "Desert Fathers." Feeling that the noise and distraction of the city had diluted their faith, these believers sold everything and moved to the desert to devote themselves to seeking God. Many thought of them as a bunch of over-zealous hermits. Yet when they returned to the cities, many were refreshed and stirred up by the simplicity and purity of their faith.

Their writings and teachings went on to form the foundation of Christian monasticism. While many followed their lead by becoming monks and nuns, even those who didn't saw the value in the periodic rhythm of leaving our busy contexts to recenter ourselves with God. Based on this tradition, foreign to me, Professor Watson instructed us to leave our context—work, school, our homes—and spend four hours in silence, solitude, and reflection.

I was resistant at first, thinking I wouldn't be able to spend four hours in some random place in complete silence. But I was also curious. What would an activity-less, phone-less, distraction-less, noise-less time do for my spirit and life? I reasoned that I needed to complete the homework assignment, so I might as well see.

To my surprise, those four hours provided me with a powerful, life-changing experience. While the first thirty minutes or so were restless and fidgety, my internal and external stressors that felt so urgent began to fade with time. My heart calmed down, and God's voice became clearer than it had been in a long time.

The longer I sat, the closer I felt to God. In my version of a "desert," I saw the patterns, pitfalls, and purposes of my daily life more clearly. I felt more certain about what changes I needed to make in my life and how I wanted to handle situations ahead. Most of all, I began to focus less on myself and more on what God was doing around me. I began asking him, "How can I be part of the story you're unfolding around me?" The result was empowering, inspirational, and invigorating.

Returning from the Desert

And then I came home.

With the enthusiasm of a child, I tried to explain this highly personal experience to my wife and friends. What words could I say? What images could I use? My words fell short of capturing the joy, clarity, and awesomeness of God. My loved ones tried to grasp what I was trying to say, but they just had to *be* there. They had to experience it for themselves. The limits of language left me feeling alone and unable to share this significant experience.

But I was determined to pursue this path. The peace I felt and the things I heard from God were unmatched in my noisy, chaotic day-to-day life. I sensed that with this one experience, I was barely scratching the surface and hungry for more.

In this pursuit, I had to reckon with my normative Christian practice. I am a fan of noisy faith, loud services, and loud prayers. I love not just loud worship; I love wild worship, with dancing and spontaneous songs that can go on for hours. But I had to reckon with the fact that while these powerful experiences produced one kind of fruit in my life, I was still missing out on the type of fruit cultivated from the quiet spaces—like on the retreat from my class assignment. I found great value in the experiential aspects of my tradition, but I could not deny that these contemplative practices were working a deep transformation inside of me that could not be found in even the biggest, wildest worship gathering.

This dichotomy began my search for a deeper understanding of spiritual practices. Not only that, but I wanted to understand how to apply them to our current challenges. I planned to take the practices of people in the third century and apply them to the twenty-first century.

To achieve these goals, I read countless Christian spiritual writers, studied the habits of my Christian forefathers and foremothers, and sought practical ways to live a more contemplative life amid a bustling metropolis.

As I integrated these practices into my life, I noticed them opening doorways for me to thrive in the midst of it. I told people about them, and I wrote about them. I taught about them. I refined and revised them repeatedly for the modern person, believing the best practices are the ones we can sustain—especially if we are living in what feels like the eye of a hurricane. These practices made me—and others I saw adopting them—more resilient, able to bounce back, adapt, and take on the challenges of the world we live in. With our internal world centered, these practices have allowed us to be more attentive to what God is doing and how we can participate in it. That is my hope for you in reading this book as well.

How to Get the Most Out of This Book

The first two chapters of this book give an overview of the paradigm, so I recommend starting there. After that, the book contains fifteen practices. These practices are grouped by the effect they can have on our lives.

The four major groupings, called "rhythms," are designed to become patterns to repeat over and over and set the tempo for how we live. The practices in each rhythm help us develop resilience in our lives in a unique way.

Depending on your needs, there are a couple of ways to read this book. One way is to read it in order. That is helpful as the rhythms build on one another. However, suppose you're in the heat of the moment with a specific need. In that case, you can also look at the

Contents page, jump to the practice that meets your immediate need, and go back to read the rest later.

Here is a breakdown of the four major rhythms that group the practices.

Rhythm One: Leaving Our Contexts (Practices 1–3)

Historically and biblically, we see that when God wants to transform people in a profound way, they are called out of their daily context for some time. This rhythm allows us to gain a new perspective, increases our dependence on God, and quiets our world so we can hear anew.

Rhythm Two: Learning to Be Still (Practices 4–6)

Once we have left, stillness provides the context in which we can begin to examine our lives. When we slow down, we can reflect on our lives, rediscover our identity apart from our efficiency, and tune into God's perspective.

Rhythm Three: Confronting Our Inner World (Practices 7–10)

Once we are reminded of who God is, this rhythm leads us to confront the root issues of our fears, anxieties, and behaviors. We learn godly ways to express anguish, address our internal wounds, and resist the temptation of division.

Rhythm Four: Returning to the World (Practices 11–15)

In the final rhythm, we prepare ourselves to return to the crazy world in which we live. Rather than living in a bubble or letting our transformation dissipate, we develop relationships that nourish us. We learn how to process the stories we hear and discover how to seek God in the heat of difficult moments. In doing so, we become part of God's greater vision for us, living faithfully and being forces of restoration in our time on earth.

In the last several years, my practice, research, framing, and teaching the practices have continued to help me stay resilient as chaos has increased. These practices have engrained rhythms in my life that allow me to meet the God who presides over chaos. I continue to gain vision, comfort, peace, and purpose in this process. My hope for this book is that it frames these chaos-proof practices in such a way that you, too, can develop rhythms of resilience in the midst of chaos.

PART 1

Our Lifeline in a Chaotic World

The Challenge of Chaos

*"Blessed is the man who trusts in the LORD, whose trust
is the LORD. He is like a tree planted by water, that sends
out its roots by the stream, and does not fear when heat
comes, for its leaves remain green, and is not anxious in
the year of drought, for it does not cease to bear fruit."*

JEREMIAH 17:7-8

I crashed onto my aisle plane seat.

I let out a loud sigh of relief as the cushion seat compressed under my weight. Even though I should have waited to see if a passenger needed the middle or window seat, I could not wait. I closed my eyes, and for a moment, just let myself rest.

I was on a flight to a long-awaited personal retreat. It was a gift from my wife, who saw the burden I was carrying in this season. Between writing a book, working a full-time job, trying to be a great husband, parenting three kids under five, training for a weightlifting competition, and leading ministries at church, I was a man running on fumes. I was physically, emotionally, and spiritually exhausted.

In addition, the past few weeks had been wrought with national crisis after crisis. It seemed the doomsday cycle on the news was never-ending. Just when people would recover from one dramatic situation, another was just around the corner. On top of my personal life, the collective anxiety of the people around me and on social media was distressing and crippling.

The days were long. My time with God was short and rushed. I longed for reprieve. A time to pray. A time to reflect. A time to seek God's face. But before I began all that, I wanted a moment to myself—some respite where no one or thing needed me. I craved enjoying the simple pleasure of an airplane soda without one of my kids asking if they could have it.

Before I could sink too deeply into this moment, in the middle of the airplane, a single, unmistakable sentence came to my mind:

Phil, you've been too busy to lead your family.

The clarity and truth of the words cut straight through me—I knew God was trying to show me something I'd been missing. It was not a voice of shame, but it convicted me with its truth. I knew what God was talking about, and I knew this was right. My life had been too chaotic to lead well. I'd been giving canned, thoughtless answers to those around me. My devotions were short and rushed, living off short readings and short prayers. Life had been moving too fast this season.

There was too much going on, and it was hampering the output of my life. Even in the craziness, I knew I was meant to be fruitful. But that had not been the case. I had been mentally or emotionally absent from my family throughout the prior few weeks. I had not cared for others how I needed to—I had been short with them. Out of my stress and anxiety, I had raised my voice or lost my temper more than I wanted to admit. I was offering everyone fifty percent of myself.

Despite the gifts God had given me and the Spirit of God living inside me, I was not thriving. I was surviving, maybe. God's message to me was: *You are not who you are meant to be when things get chaotic in your life.*

Hearing God Speak

In this book, I share many stories where I believe God was leading me. While I go deeper into this idea in the practice of Intentional Listening, I wanted to touch on it here, as it can be a somewhat mysterious subject.

As we look through our scripture, tradition, and community, we see that people experience God's leading in a variety of ways. Typically, when we use the phrase "hearing God's voice," we use "hearing" as a metaphor to describe a sense of divine communication that defies our language. Often, this comes as a timely insight, thought, word, scripture, or image, etc. that resonates with a certain meaning in our spirit. It also seems to have originated outside our natural human thought. These experiences often give us new strength, wisdom, guidance, comfort, passion, or revelation.

I share my stories with God knowing we can never know the fullness of God's perspective while we're here on earth. However, believing God desires to speak to us, we can listen and test the impressions we receive against scripture, God's character, and with others in our community to discern if what we're "hearing" is on base. The stories I share here have been tested in those ways. I hope they encourage you and clarify how God may also lead you.

This book is about faith practices that help us thrive in times of chaos.

Whenever I tell someone I'm writing this book, I get the same response. Every. Single. Time. Their eyes widen, they nod slowly, and they momentarily vanish into another world. What provokes them is the word "chaos." They stare blankly into space and slowly nod. "Yes, we need that in these times."

We each have a unique association with the word chaos. You might think of your crazy week at work, a project running late, or the work you take home after hours. Or you may be a parent with young kids, thinking about the morning yelling match to get in the car with a piece of toast half hanging from their mouths—I've been there before.

If you're a church leader, you may think of the demands of the church, the drama and difficulty of relationships within it, and the wild ups and downs of services. If you're in one of the many vicious, never-ending, end-of-the-world news cycles, you may think of the latest disaster, political turmoil, or social unrest. While the specifics of our chaos may differ, we look at each with understanding eyes saying, "Yes, we live in a crazy world."

I know what comes to mind when I think about that word. I think about juggling work, family, relationships, ministry, and writing. I'm reminded of the ongoing conflicts, potential threats, and social issues of our time. It seems like there is turmoil everywhere we look.

As much as I would like to point fingers over how bad our world has gotten in recent years, there were many times I was not in a good place myself. At times, I was depressed, angry, and behaved as anything but a pillar of peace. I always nod back to those who nod at me. With a heavy sigh and eyes of empathy, I say, "Yes, chaos is troublesome."

The Believer's Challenge in Chaos

Chaos and distress aren't the exceptions anymore; they are the norm. It seems we've come to expect it, both in our personal lives and in the public arena. There doesn't seem to be a week we are not combatting some personal or global tumult.

What is it about chaos that is so troublesome? What about its presence in our lives makes having a thriving spirituality difficult? I see the struggle of believers in our generation framed through this passage in Mark 4:37–40.

> A great windstorm arose, and the waves were breaking into the boat so that the boat was already filling. But he was in the stern, asleep on the cushion. And they woke him and said to him, "Teacher, do you not care that we are perishing?" And he awoke and rebuked the wind and said to the sea, "Peace! Be still!" And the wind ceased, and there was a great calm. He said to them, "Why are you so afraid? Have you still no faith?" And they were filled with great fear and said to one another, "Who then is this, that even the wind and the sea obey him?"

A storm begins raging as the disciples and Jesus go to sea. The disciples see the storm coming, and they feel the wind growing in strength. Perhaps the sound of thunder is rumbling across the horizon. Lightning pierces the sky. They cling to each other, looking around. "What do we do?!" Here they were, helpless at the mercy of the storm.

In a panic, they go down to the stern and find Jesus. He's their leader, their teacher—he'll know what to do. But what is he doing? They find him sleeping, of course. How can Jesus sleep in all this? With the boat lurching back and forth, icy spray wetting his clothes, the voices calling out in panic? What peace does one have that makes one sleep in the middle of the storm? Does he know something they don't?

They shout to wake him, "Don't you care that we are perishing?"

He sits up. Maybe he rubs some sleep from his eyes. Then, to the disciples' shock, Jesus speaks to the storm. "Be still!" The storm listens to him. The boat returns to its gentle sway. The disciples stand in awe. Who is this Jesus?

Something happens in that passage that convicts me. I think what's shocking isn't that Jesus calmed the storm. It isn't that they survived. It's that Jesus asks them, "Why are you afraid?" He challenges their response of fear. He says, "You of little faith!"

He wants them to know better. "Don't you know, guys? Don't you know who I am?" In their fear, they forgot some important details about Jesus. They forgot that he made the storm and the sea. Of course, Jesus can calm the sea! They forgot that Jesus was the Word of God who spoke all things into creation. They forgot that the God of the universe was traveling in the same boat as them. Compared to the size of the storm, the size of Jesus's power far outweighed whatever storm they faced.

When we are afraid, we fixate on the clouds, rain, and howling wind, which overshadow our minds and thinking. Like drowning in a pool, all we can think about is surviving. In that moment, the disciples lost sight of the capable hands in which they could rest. In similar circumstances, we can develop anxiety, fear and worry by fixating on the world around us. Like the disciples, we forget that God is with us and He is greater than the storms of life.

That is the believer's problem in chaos. The bigger the waves around us grow, the more disoriented we can become. As we become more disoriented, the following are the dominoes that fall:

1. Chaos disconnects us from God.

What is a branch without its trunk? A withering one. So is the Christian who's disconnected. Jesus said in John 15, "I am the vine, you are the branches." Our ability to thrive is dependent on our ongoing connection to the vine.

When chaos comes, it jeopardizes the precious connection we have with God. We as humans tend to focus on the loudest, brightest thing happening. We gaze on its effect and impact. Like watching a national crisis unfold on television, we cannot divert our eyes. Or we become entranced by the tasks and problems before us that feel most urgent. The chaos and its effects can dominate our minds. It distracts us with its rage and deafens us with its siren.

Like a tree trying to stay upright against potent winds, chaos places our relationship with God on tenuous ground. We get too busy to stop and listen. We shortchange our spiritual practices and lose connection with our local faith communities.

That is the first and most significant domino of chaos. There is no skill, talent, or financial advantage that helps people more than their connection with God. When that is lost, it starts a domino effect that topples the other elements in our lives.

> When chaos comes, it jeopardizes the precious connection we have with God.

2. Chaos brings internal despair.

When we lose track of God, our internal equilibrium is lost. We enter a rocky mental, emotional, and spiritual state. I've felt the sting of this many times. There have been weeks where chaos, personal or otherwise, has been so loud that my sense of peace is lost.

This loss of peace manifests in stress, anxiety, and worry. It's hard to think clearly, and it becomes difficult to make rational and peaceful choices. We can easily lash out at people through our emotional angst and anxiety. Ultimately, our world operates off-center, and without reconnecting to center us, we continue to grow further and further off-course.

3. Chaos leads us to cause further disruption.

Perhaps the trickiest effect of chaos is that it tends to make us part of the problem. Instead of being agents of light, salt, and peace—as we are called to be as Christians—we are at risk of adding to the chaos around us.

Unless we have practices to stay connected to God, the fruit of our lives will be a byproduct of everything we take in from the world around us. We start to just go through the motions or follow the crowd instead of being in control of our spiritual lives.

Jesus said we would know a tree by its fruit. If the inside of us is chaotic and distressed, what comes out of us will inevitably follow suit. We are not peacemakers but contribute to the noise, vitriol, anger, stress, and anxiety. We recognize this is incongruent with our calling as Christians. We are called to be light in the darkest places, but we can lose track of that light inside of ourselves.

Spiritual resilience is the key to thriving in chaos. But it begs the question: how do we become resilient? We do not become resilient by intellectual thought or accident. Rather, we must grow our roots so deep and wide that it doesn't matter what happens in our lives—we can stay connected to God and be fruitful.

Faith Practices for Spiritual Resilience

How do we Christians handle all the chaos in our personal lives and the public sector?

One day, I had an insight into this question while on a hike in the Sierra Nevada Mountains. Despite a dry California, greenery surrounded me—shrubs, vines, and trees everywhere. High rocks stood on my right and left, so it felt almost like walking through a tunnel but with an open top. The sun could only be seen in the narrow strip when it passed directly overhead. Because the rock formations only let the sun through the passage directly overhead, most of the greenery was on the floor. At the same time, the walls of the mountain to my side lay bare.

Midway through the hike, I saw something that stopped me in my tracks. Perched upon one of the barren mountainous walls were a small set of trees. Unlike the trees on the floor where they could receive sunlight, the mountain perpetually shaded these trees. In response, they grew entirely sideways. Their trunks were parallel to the ground. You could grab onto their trunks like monkey bars and hang from them. Because they grew sideways, their leaves could reach where the sunlight shone.

I stopped walking to marvel at this sight. I saw myself in these trees. Sometimes I feel like my life doesn't follow the norm. I feel like the exception to the rule, the one with extra challenges. Yet for these trees, despite the location, lack of sun, and a wind tunnel, their root systems dug deep into the soil of the mountainside and clung on. The trees adapted and overcame great obstacles to reach sunlight.

The trees that survived and even thrived did so because they were resilient.

Similarly, the challenge for Christians living in these chaotic times is to develop resilience. Typically, resilience is defined as being adaptable and flexible, able to recover quickly from difficulty.

> I would define spiritual resilience this way: "The ability to adjust our spiritual lives to stay connected to God so we thrive in even the most challenging circumstances."

Pursuing resilience is key to our thriving spirituality for at least two noteworthy reasons. The first is that it doesn't pretend chaos isn't present. Resilience is not a call to dig our heads in the sand and wish it away. It isn't hiding our Christian existence while the world rages. Instead, when we pursue resilience, we assume chaos will come. We expect it, and we prepare.

Second, pursuing resilience calls us higher. It requires us to adapt—not just our approach or our thinking, but our very selves. I believe God uses chaos in our lives to sharpen us, shape us, and mold us into people more like Christ. Ultimately, the pursuit of spiritual resilience forms us into the people we are meant to be in this world.

What Does Spiritual Resilience Look Like?

What does it look like for us to be spiritually resilient? Those trees, flourishing out of the side of the mountain, can teach us quite a bit about how this manifests in our lives.

1. Spiritual resilience means being adaptable to find the light (God).

The sideways trees had great obstacles to reaching what gave them life. They had to go against gravity to do so, literally. They insisted upon gaining access to the sun, twisting upward to reach nourishment. With the sun's vital energy, the trees could extend their branches and expand themselves.

In the same way, chaos puts us in all sorts of precarious situations where God is hard to find. Despite the environment challenging our spiritual lives, we must learn how to adapt the approaches we have historically relied upon and find God in uncertain terrain.

2. Spiritual resilience means staying attached.

It is one thing to be rooted. It is a whole different thing to *stay* rooted.

Imagine a young seed being blown up the side of the mountain and grabbing on for dear life, roots rapidly pushing into the soil. In defiance of gravity, the root system would have to grow deep and strong enough to keep the tree attached to the mountainside.

Resilience for us means having our spiritual roots attached so firmly that no matter what blows our way, we do not lose our connection with God. It means whatever craziness life throws at us, as long as we strive to keep our relationship with God intact, we can continue to draw life from the source.

3. Spiritual resilience means bearing fruit.

At the top of the sideways trees were branches spread wide, full of luscious green leaves and acorns. They were just as fruitful as any other tree in the forest.

Fruitful means they grow fruit that people can enjoy, and in turn, the fruit nourishes them. Whether it is the fruit of our lives, words, actions, ministry, or presence, the Lord promises our lives can be so healthy as to nourish not only ourselves but others as well. Yes, that means even in a "year of drought"—especially then, since everyone will be searching for water. When our world's leaders and heroes falter, the people of God can bear fruit even when no one else is. And in the words of Jesus in John 15:8, we can bear "much" fruit.

A tree well-rooted cares not about the wind. It does not worry about the storm, fire, nor winds. It is confident and certain. It is so sure that its roots can withstand what is to come, it laughs and scoffs in the face of peril. That is the approach we must harness. We can receive God's presence and strength to overcome those obstacles and live lives of abundance, albeit unconventional, or coming out of the side of the mountain.

Jesus Sets the Example

Jesus came to earth to change the entire axis of the world through his sacrifice on the cross and the raising up of the church. Yet he only had three years to do it. Talk about a time-sensitive endeavor. Every week, day, and decision counted.

Jesus didn't only face the pressure of time but also the pressure of people around him. He was a walking miracle. He healed the sick, raised the dead, ministered to the poor, and changed the destiny of thousands and thousands of people. As much as we feel time pressure—project deadlines, problem-solving, family development milestones, we will never deal with what Jesus encountered.

While he is the Son of God, he was, on earth, also human, like us. He felt stressed tired, and hungry, and he grew frustrated at people. The way he navigated these pressures is a model for us as our pressures increase.

While Christians typically pay attention to the result of what Jesus did, not everyone pays attention to the rhythms of life that made his actions possible. When the pressure was on, he consistently did certain things that allowed him to withstand a severe load, see his Father clearly, and make faithful moves.

So what were the things that allowed Jesus to thrive?

1. Jesus regularly left his context.
2. He took time to be still.
3. He confronted his inner world in prayer.
4. He returned to his context to take his next faithful step.

We will explore examples of each throughout this book. These patterns served Jesus whether he needed to recharge, make a decision, work through emotions, or prepare for what was ahead. These rhythms allowed God's hand to move freely in and through him even when the stakes were highest. The rhythms in this book are based on these four patterns.

Faith Practices That Help Us Become More Resilient

I'm presenting fifteen practices that can help people of faith develop rhythms of resilience, especially in times of crisis. These practices have all left a mark on my life, and I have found them invaluable in my faith journey to become resilient. They have several unique features that make them effective when the times are tumultuous:

1. They counteract the specific effects of chaos.

Chaos leaves its mark on us in a variety of ways, making it difficult to discern the solution. As the doctor would suggest, we need to take the right medicine for the right problem. These practices tackle specific effects chaos has on our lives. They allow us to get to the root of the problem versus applying a broad solution hoping something sticks.

> These rhythms are like a rudder of a ship. It only takes this small device to pivot and turn something that's hundreds and thousands of tons. The faith practices we give ourselves have the power to determine the trajectory of our lives.

2. They help us escape a spiral.

Chaos is often like a whirlwind. It's a fast-moving force in our lives that can usher us to a bad place. Perhaps we've seen what we become when we allow that to happen, or we see where it has taken others. We don't want to be caught in its vicious spiral. The power of these practices is that they help us take an immediate step out of the spiral.

3. They allow us to reach God, even from a dark place.

Spiritual practices are critical in chaos precisely because you don't have to have your act together to do them. On the contrary, these are designed for when we are in our worse state. They are both simple enough for a child and powerful enough to change your future. Despite not feeling like doing them, not knowing how to do them, or even doing them with wrong intentions, they must be the cornerstone of public and personal faith.

These rhythms are like a rudder of a ship. It only takes this small device to pivot and turn something that's hundreds and thousands of tons. The faith practices we give ourselves have the power to determine the trajectory of our lives.

4. They position us to be transformed.

Our foremost resource is God. These spiritual practices themselves do not transform us. Rather, they position us to be transformed by God's Spirit, who works mysteriously and miraculously in us. We believe that as we give ourselves over to them, God will give us what we need to be fruitful and resilient in chaos.

Spiritual practices are the center of the Christian life. They allow us to meet with God and grow spiritually. But we've learned that we need specific rhythms to help us when things get crazy. The fifteen practices written in this book help us to do precisely that. In the process, we follow the footsteps of Jesus and all the biblical heroes who found God in their great times of need and upheaval. The resilience we develop allows us to participate in the story of healing and restoration God is writing in our time.

PART 2

Faith Practices for Building Resilience in Chaos

Leaving Our Contexts

*We must go out into a desert of some kind (your
backyard will do) and come into a personal
experience of the incredible love of God.*
BRENNAN MANNING

*You are at your best when you are alone with God. That's
probably true of every Christian to one degree or another.*
DEE HENDERSON, TRACES OF GUILT

Once there were two tree choppers. Being proud of their talent, they decided to have a contest one day to see who could chop the most trees within a single day. Both eagerly agreed to the competition, and they commenced the next day.

The first tree chopper hit the ground running, chopping away furiously. He could hear the second tree chopper chopping away at a distance. As he continued to chop tree after tree, he noticed that every so often, the sound of chopping from the second tree chopper would stop for a short time.

"This is my time to get ahead," the first chopper thought to himself. Motivated by the pause of the second chopper, he would chop even harder. The day went on, and this would happen again and again. He would hear a pause, laugh to himself, and continue chopping.

By the end of the day and the competition, the two tree choppers reconvened and compared their work. Much to the first tree chopper's surprise and chagrin, the second tree chopper had cut significantly more trees than the first.

Taken aback, the first tree chopper demanded to know how this was the case. "How did you manage to chop more trees than me? Every time you took a break, I continued to chop more. By simple math, it stands to reason that I would have chopped more. What did you do when you stopped chopping?"

Admiring his axe as he held it up, the second tree chopper turned to him, smiled, and said, "I was sharpening my ax."

Daily, it's easy to find ourselves chopping away. It seems there's always a task to accomplish, a deadline to meet, soccer practice to attend, or a gathering to host.

Do you relate to this scenario? Do you run nonstop from one thing to the next with no space between them? Are you moving at such great speed and consistency that the events start to feel all the same? From deadlines to date night, when we move so fast, everything on our plate can blur into something we no longer recognize.

In this fast-paced mindset, it's easy to treat even the moments meant to be savored as another task to accomplish. We toss it into the "done" pile so we can get to the next thing because we're always running behind. We feel the pressure of the clock—maybe even the pressure others experience, or so we think.

In American society, productivity is one of our highest values. And yet, it's uncommon to think that perhaps the most productive thing we could do is stop and take a step back.

But like the tree chopper who never stopped, we think the best way to catch up, or even get ahead, is to continue to push. We may blame ourselves for falling behind, wishing we had what it took to handle it, go faster, and carry more. Whether it's the chaos of our jobs, families, or ministries, we often wish we had what it takes to thrive in it.

It's typical to believe that there's this one missing piece and look outside of ourselves to find it. Many of us wish we had more resources to make chaos more manageable. If only we had more money. More network. A better job. Even more time. Is there anything you find yourself wishing you had more of? It's tempting to think those things would help.

But what if that missing piece isn't within our reach right now? Must we wait to be at peace until a new job offer falls in our lap? Even if it did, how do we know it would solve all our problems? It's easy to get so caught up wishing things would get easier that we forget what's already at our disposal.

One of the greatest resources to help us in chaos is our ability to develop resilience. That is not a self-help mantra. That is the way God consistently prepares people to thrive in chaotic situations. More often than changing the circumstance we're in, God chooses to change us in it and through it. It is changed people who change the world.

How does God shape, form, and prepare this resilience in us? As we see in the life of Jesus, the first step is withdrawing from our context.

> How does God shape, form, and prepare this resilience in us? As we see in the life of Jesus, the first step is withdrawing from our context.

I didn't realize withdrawing could be a spiritual practice until I started doing so myself. Although initially uncomfortable, I was utterly blown away by the experience. Even though my life was becoming increasingly hectic, I felt God gave me clarity and courage in critical areas of my life where I was struggling. I came back charged and filled with purpose. All from a few hours of being away? Unbelievable.

After this experience, I couldn't help but notice something. Leaving his context wasn't just something Jesus did once at the very beginning of his ministry, but he made a habit of it.

- In Luke 4:1–2, 14–15, Jesus retreats to spend forty days praying in the wilderness after being baptized and before his public ministry begins.

- In Luke 6:12–13, Jesus spends the whole night alone in prayer before choosing his twelve disciples.

- In Mark 6:30–32, after sending his disciples out for ministry, he encourages them to retreat alone and rest.

- In Luke 15:16 and many other instances, Jesus retreats to spend time alone in prayer.

- In Luke 22: 39–44, shortly before he is to be arrested, Jesus goes to the Mt. of Olives and prays alone in agony over what he will soon face.

As I mentioned, Jesus's ministry was incredibly hectic. He had the daunting task of changing the world in just three and a half years. As news of his ministry and miracles spread, he was under constant pressure and attention. Like a celebrity in our modern age, countless people scrutinized him, asked things of him, and plotted against him.

If we were in his shoes, the pressure might break us. With such a great weight on our shoulders, we may be driven to endless self-criticism. We may lash out at those who need us. "Can't I just have one moment alone?" We may feel bitterness toward those who judge us and try to retaliate. I'd likely clam up at all the difficult questions he was asked. The power and fame could go to our heads, leading us to compromising decisions. Or we might be tempted to run away and never come back.

Yet Jesus did not do any of these things. No matter what was going on in Jesus's ministry, no matter how busy things got, how many people needed him, or how great things were going, he withdrew. He withdrew regularly. He went away when he was needed most. He retreated when everyone was looking for him. He took some time off alone. He disengaged even from those closest to him.

He didn't just withdraw as a form of escape. When he came back, he became a person ready to tackle the crazy. It was Jesus's strategy as a human.

Beyond Jesus' life, this pattern is evident throughout the Old Testament, New Testament, and Christian history. Moses was developed for forty years in the wilderness before returning to Egypt. Jonah was shaped and sharpened in the belly of the fish before preaching to Nineveh. Elijah was sent to the mountain's cleft before returning to speak to the wayward kings of Israel. David spent decades wandering mountains and caves before taking the kingship. In these "away" spaces, God equipped each of these figures with tools for when they'd return.

How Leaving Creates Resilience

It's tempting to feel that if we step away from the grindstone, everything will fall apart. We may believe by continuing to stay at home, work, or in ministry 24/7, we can prevent mistakes, avoid failure, move faster, and avoid letting anyone down. Yet like the tree chopper who never stopped to sharpen his axe, our constant presence can be a disservice to our long-term goals and calling.

When we don't have rhythms of withdrawal, we rob ourselves of the transformation God does inside of us. We deny his formative hand in our lives that enables us to thrive in chaos. Here's how leaving counteracts chaos's pressure toward constant motion.

1. Leaving sharpens our ability to see God's perspective.

Too often, in chaos, we get buried. And when we get buried, we can only see so much. We make reactive, short-term decisions and lose track of the larger picture. For example, I struggle with getting frustrated at my kids in the heat of the moment, so I forget the larger vision of disciplining them well. I make an emotional decision to buy something but neglect the larger vision of stewarding my finances.

When lost in a forest, the first thing we need to do is find the high ground. When we withdraw, the foreground of our context fades away, and we can start seeing things from afar. Like standing on a tall rock in the middle of a forest, we can see patterns we didn't see before. We can see pathways previously not in our view. We have the vantage point to make decisions out of the big picture.

Leaving versus Avoidance

Chaos often triggers fear, and one common response to fear is our "flight" instinct or the instinct to escape from what's causing us stress. Escaping or avoidance can look like the spiritual practice of withdrawing, but I want to clarify that they're not the same.

Flight, escape, or avoidance is a physical, chemical response to fear in our brains. In genuinely dangerous situations, this saves us. Yet in situations that aren't actually dangerous (stress at work, tension with a friend), avoidance becomes an unhelpful habit that keeps us from resolving our problems.

Rather than a fear response, the rhythm of leaving is an intentional habit. Tightly coupled with reflection, the practice of leaving can give us the insight we couldn't have gained had we stayed. Withdrawing helps to recenter ourselves so we can return to our context better equipped to handle it the way Jesus would.

2. Leaving sharpens our ability to see miracles in chaos.

When we've been in the same context for too long, we develop a paradigm for what's possible and not based on what we've seen before. Our brains can become accustomed to the cycle of doom. We lack the imagination to see how things could be different.

Often, I have claimed to still believe in miracles, reconciliation, healing, and a move of God. Still, if I'm honest, I didn't expect it to happen just because I hadn't seen it happen before. We can become like the Israelites when they clung to slavery in Egypt simply because it was their norm. When we're caught in what *is* and *has been*, we can become blind to what *could be*.

It is particularly frustrating when God wants to do great things in our chaotic situations, and he wants to do it with us. Our chaotic workplaces, ministries, and home lives are so often in need of miracles!

Leaving our context shakes off the blinders of normalcy. We can partner with God to see "impossible" things when we remove these blinders.

3. Leaving sharpens our closeness to God.

Have you ever seen two people fall in love on a mission trip? This has become a common and humorous trope in many Christian circles, but I think it points to a simple truth about humans: when we're in an unfamiliar situation, we press into what's familiar. Overseas, people navigate a world of uncomfortable, unfamiliar territory together. Overcoming that discomfort with another person breeds a unique form of intimacy. I believe the same principle applies to our relationship with God.

We often find ourselves drawing closer to God when we're in uncomfortable, unfamiliar contexts. We press in because we need him more there, but out of that need grows a deeper intimacy with him. Just like when the Spirit sent Jesus to the desert, God was his only source of comfort and strength. Similarly, David wrote heart-wrenchingly intimate Psalms while running from Saul. Elijah experienced God's intimate whisper while being hunted. In the discomfort of leaving our contexts—by choice or by force—we can discover a new form of connection. This connection is grounding to us in a world bent on disconnecting us from God's presence and mission.

Three Practices for Leaving

We need rhythms of leaving that enable us to be sharpened. So how can we practice this rhythm of withdrawing from our contexts? In the next chapters, I will present three practices to make leaving a regular rhythm in our lives.

Practice 1: Prayer Walk (Daily)
Practice 2: Micro-Retreat (Weekly)
Practice 3: Personal Retreat (Seasonal)

Prayer Walk: The Daily Rejuvenator

*Smart men walked on the moon, daring men walked
on the ocean floor, but wise men walk with God.*
LEONARD RAVENHILL

My heart was pounding. I felt indignant, confused, angry, and hurt.

I just got out of a meeting with a colleague who went AWOL. After months of working well together, with a single email, they completely turned their back on me and threw me under the bus. *How could they?*

With my keyboard in hand and SAT vocabulary at my disposal, I was ready to write the vengeance email of a lifetime. *Wait till they read this.* I had all my counterpoints ready to fire.

Just before I hit send, a piece of advice from an old manager intruded upon my thoughts: "Never send an email angrily." Even though I was seething, I took that advice. Instead, I did what I knew I needed to do—I took a Prayer Walk.

I didn't know where I was going. I just stormed out the door and started walking. I did my best impression of King David and started whining to God. *Can't you see what they wrote about me? Can you believe what they said?*

The more I walked, the more I noticed certain changes. Though subtle at first, they became more apparent as minutes passed. I noticed the edges of my emotions weren't as sharp. I observed that it was a gorgeous day—the sun was shining on my face. It was as if God's presence was there to say, "I'm here. It's going to be okay." After calming myself, I began asking God for wisdom. "God, how should I respond? What are you thinking?" I circled the corner, heading back to the office.

Within a few minutes, an idea came to mind for another way to respond. I became aware of an angle of the situation I didn't see before. As I headed back into the office, the words of anger and justice were no longer necessary. Instead, I felt that God had equipped me with words of wisdom, grace, and tact.

I sat down, placed my hands on the keyboard, and wrote a much different letter than the original.

Potential stressors fill our days. And in that atmosphere, losing our connection with God and our center is easy. How do we center ourselves in the middle of a crazy day? Sometimes, we need something to help us *right now*, when we only have a couple of minutes to gather ourselves and respond. This is where the Prayer Walk comes in. What is a Prayer Walk?

> *The Prayer Walk is a five to twenty-five minute practice of leaving our contexts midday to restore our soul in prayerful connection with God.*

The Power of the Prayer Walk

Reflecting on my years of practicing the Prayer Walk, I have concluded that there are three main reasons why it's such a powerful tool in our arsenal as Christians.

1. This walk reduces stress in God-designed ways.

God designed us as *whole* people—mind, body, and spirit wrapped into one. I don't think it's an accident that moving our bodies is a way to help our brains reduce stress and recenter us. Physical exercise like walking is proven to release endorphins, chemically reducing stress in the human body. Even after a ten-minute brisk walk, our body sends the signals to reduce the stress and anxiety we may have been feeling. Harvard Health even reported that walking reduced stress regardless of the time of day or weather (unless you're walking in the middle of a tornado).[1] So whatever time of day it is, whether the weather is perfect or not, go for it. It's a double blessing God designed and baked right into the Prayer Walk practice.

> God designed us as *whole* people—mind, body, and spirit wrapped into one. I don't think it's an accident that moving our bodies is a way to help our brains reduce stress and recenter us.

2. This walk allows God-given creative thinking for hard problems.

A Christian therapist friend once told me, "People need to be in a position where they can catch a breath before they can help solve a problem." He taught me that when people experience fear, their brains cannot think critically. In these moments, we either fight, freeze or flee. The part of our brain that thinks critically, empathizes, and solves problems is shut down so it can focus on protecting us from perceived danger.

The converse is also true. We can problem-solve when we are relaxed. In fact, our best problem-solving occurs when we're not thinking about the problem at all!

You may have noticed that you can focus attention on a troublesome situation, but clarity won't come to your conscious mind. So, you give up and go about your day. Suddenly, when you're in the shower, driving to the market, or watching television, and voila! The answer comes to you when you least expect it.

This occurs because even when you're not actively problem-solving, your brain doesn't shut off. When we ask ourselves questions like, "What should I do next?" or "How could I see this differently?" our subconscious mind is listening. Our conscious attention may move on to deal with other things, but the subconscious continues to ponder these questions.[2] Then, it pops into your consciousness when it figures out a possible solution. The Prayer Walk gives our attention something new to focus on so our subconscious brain can work on the problems we've yet to solve.

3. The walk creates a space for simple, honest prayer.

Our environment changes the type of conversations people have. I have very different conversations with my wife depending on whether we're on a date, we're bussing the kids around, or we're just driving. Our environment changes the formality, intimacy, and content of our conversations.

The same is typically true of our conversations with God. Some of us are accustomed to talking with God in formal spaces. However, the people we walk and talk with are our friends. Walking with God invites the conversation to follow our stream of consciousness rather than something tidy and routine. The prayers and conversations we can have with God are casual, intimate, and relaxed. We can share openly from our hearts, talk about random things, and genuinely enjoy God's presence in a way that allows our emotions to cool and puts our spirit in a better place.

How to Practice the Prayer Walk

Step 1: Start walking.

Get in a different environment. It doesn't need to be anywhere extravagant. It can be down the hallway from your office or stepping into your backyard. Don't overcomplicate it—step away from the physical location where you are experiencing the stress.

Once you're there, start walking. Leave your devices behind. Let it be just you and God. Enjoy the world around you. I try to breathe slowly and pay attention to my breath moving in and out of my lungs. It allows me to stop thinking intensely about whatever is occupying my mind and be completely present in this activity.

Step 2: Decompress with God.

It is hard to come up with meaningful conversations when you're stressed. Well, I have good news for you–don't feel pressured to speak eloquently. Many of the Psalms are simple cries of a broken-hearted person. Our prayers don't need to make sense; they need to be honest.

Speak from your heart to God. Tell him what's on your mind or what you see around you. This is a time to decompress and speak honestly.

Note: If you're experiencing deep grief, trauma, rage, or sorrow, read the chapter on the practice of "Holy Lament." It may be a moment to lament your frustration before figuring out what to do next.

Step 3: Ask for God's perspective.

After you've decompressed, it's important to seek a deeper understanding of what God is doing in the moment. First, in the short walk, I try to spend some time asking, "Lord, what are you saying about this situation?" It's a simple question. I want to know God's thoughts, feelings, and opinions about what I'm going through. I know I'm probably stuck in the trees, but God sees and created the forest. As I continue walking, I remain attentive to any new insight or clarity that may come.

What was the last thing God told me?

I believe that when God speaks, it is timely. I have often read a piece of scripture or listened to a sermon, but I didn't understand its application in the moment. However, it turned out to be exactly what I needed the following day, week, or even year. God used it to prepare me for what I couldn't yet see. For this reason, I will often try to remember the last thing I felt God told me and ask for insight on how it applies to my present circumstance.

Step 4: Ask God for help.

The next step is to ask for help. It doesn't have to be complicated or verbose. Pray a simple prayer like:

Lord, help me.
Give me wisdom.
Show me what to say.

Note: Consider reading the chapter on One-Second Prayers as another tool for your walks.

> ### Intercessory Prayer Walk
>
> Many have used the Prayer Walk as a space to pray for the things we see around us during our walk. Missionaries have famously walked the neighborhoods of their area praying for every house, for people they see, for neighborhoods, and for schools or businesses they pass. Integrate this if you feel inspired to do so. It often serves to take our focus off the specific scenario in front of us and remember that we are actively involved in the bigger picture of what God is doing around us.

Step 5: Return.

Come back to the place where you started. If you felt like God showed you something new on your walk, or if a word, phrase, or image came to mind that comforted you, write it down. If you believe God gave you the next step to take, go forward with it.

In the busyness of the day, the Prayer Walk is a powerful, accessible tool to help us decompress, reconnect, and move forward. If you're finding yourself drowning, overwhelmed, or highly stressed, take a Prayer Walk. The daily walk is an easy way to practice the rhythm of withdrawing.

Micro-Retreat:
The Weekly Recentering

We live in a world that is beyond our control, and life is in a constant flux of change. So we have a decision to make: keep trying to control a storm that is not going to go away or start learning how to live within the rain.

GLENN PEMBERTON, HURTING WITH GOD

I received the task of going on a retreat as part of another seminary class. It was in a Franciscan retreat center in Malibu, California. I walked up to the weathered white and red brick building and breathed in the salty air. There were countless walking paths with tall trees shading me overhead. I soaked in the intriguing statues and gorgeous view overlooking the ocean below. As I wandered about the grounds, every muscle in my body relaxed.

I had three days of complete silence, solitude, and deep prayer before God. I was so rejuvenated. I felt connected to God, had a sense of clarity about what he was doing in my life, and perceived that I could see the arc of where he wanted to take me.

Then I went home. An important question formed in my mind. "Why can't I do this all the time?" And then my daughter threw an egg at the wall, a pile of bills landed on my desk, my wife told me we need to meal plan for the next week, and we had guests coming over in an hour. "Oh yeah, that's why." I sighed deeply.

While getting away for a few days revitalizes our mind, body, and spirit, it's not realistic to do so every week. Or even every month. I'm lucky if I can do it a few times a year, and I do try. But I loved the person I was after the retreat. I had difficulty accepting that I could only have that level of clarity and revitalization a few times a year or when I went to Malibu. I needed to get more creative. I figured I might not have two or three days, but if I applied the same principles over several hours, surely I could get *something* out of it. That birthed what I call a Weekly Micro-Retreat. What is a Micro-Retreat?

> A Micro-Retreat is a roughly two- to four-hour block during the week where one can leave their everyday context to connect deeply with God and care for their soul.

Often, when people realize they need to combat chaos, it's too late. Life feels like it's collapsing on them. I've been there before, and it's not fun. This method is preventative. This practice anticipates and equips us for the chaos to come.

I practice the Micro-Retreat once a week, and it has become a fixture in my life. Every weekend, my wife and I will respectively and individually leave our home (our context) for a few hours at a time. We find a place where we can unplug—a time where we can reflect, journal, engage in silence, and pray. The Micro-Retreat is easier to plan and implement than an overnight trip or a whole day, but it's still long enough to center ourselves for the upcoming week. In the thick of parenting, work, busy ministry seasons, and national crises, this weekly Micro-Retreat has helped us tremendously. It has helped us stay focused, get plugged into God, and to come out with purpose and revelation.

The Power of the Micro-Retreat

Here are a few components that make this practice so effective:

1. A change of context brings a fresh perspective to our faith.

As discussed in the previous chapter, location is everything. In chaos, people tend to hunker down and stay put. Our familiarity leaves us with huge blind spots that we cannot even begin to deconstruct because we can't see them. As a result, we lose perspective, we can't discern what needs to change, and we lose our sense of where God is in it. Intentionally going somewhere else to seek God and clarity gives us the distance needed to see from a new perspective.

2. The length of time allows us to focus on what's important rather than what's immediate.

The most urgent things consume our attention when we're in the grind. Maybe it's the email we need to send, the fire to put out at work, the homework assignment, the bill to pay, or the screaming child.

When we leave, we can devote attention to bigger-picture things God may have for us. We can evaluate how we've been spending our lives and ensure we've aligned with the big-picture calling. We can remember important things we've forgotten because they were not urgent or screaming in our faces. We catch wind of God's dreams and vision for our lives and what we need to do to move closer to them.

3. This space allows us to work multiple "spiritual muscles" at once.

If you're trying to build muscle all over, you don't want an exercise that works one muscle. You want an exercise that strengthens multiple muscles at a time. Especially when we don't have a lot of time to exercise in our schedule, these types of exercises maximize our time. In the same way, Micro-Retreats are a way to string together multiple practices in a nice package. You can fill in the time with other practices from this book.

4. Practicing this weekly or biweekly matches our natural cadence.

Most everyone I talk to has a natural weekly cadence. We have a week of work or school and a natural break. This practice fits nicely into a typical weekly rhythm. Instead of trudging onward, missing out on a precious opportunity to reflect, this is a great time to look back at our crazy week. As we look back, we reconnect to ourselves and can comprehend how God is moving in our lives.

Furthermore, many people who practice this spend considerable time looking forward. My wife loves this time to organize her week, pray through upcoming events, and hear God's voice for the challenges ahead. It allows us to feel ready and spiritually tuned for the week to come.

How to Practice the Micro-Retreat

Step 1: Find a multi-hour window you can block out in your calendar.

It takes time for our soul to slow down, it takes time to go deep, and it takes time to think, reflect, and pray. One hour isn't quite sufficient for this. If anything goes wrong—parking, finding a spot, a phone call, etc.—a large part of your time is already gone. Too long, and it ends up bleeding into other responsibilities, creating additional stress.

The sweet spot for me is around two to four hours. As you practice this, you will find your own sweet spot. If this is your first time, I recommend planning for two hours.

> It takes time for our soul to slow down, it takes time to go deep, and it takes time to think, reflect, and pray.

Step 2: Choose the location.

Plan to be outside your daily context. Your location could be a park, coffee shop, garden, library, beach, etc. Here are some suggestions on what to look for in a location:

- Find a place that is quiet
- Find a spot where you can be alone
- Find somewhere as far as you can (Maybe that means your backyard, but if you can go farther, go for it!)
- Find places of nature

I enjoy places where I can walk and pray and sit and reflect, like a garden or a local park. I will drive to a mountainous area and sit in my car if nothing else is available.

Step 3: Plan what it will take to guard this time.

Does taking a Micro-Retreat on Saturday mean you must finish all your work on Friday? Does it mean you need your spouse to take the kids for a few hours or find childcare? Do you need to let anyone know you won't be available during that time? Do you need to get to sleep earlier or block out a different time in the week to accomplish a task?

Life will press in on this time. If we don't plan for it, we will either: 1) abandon our responsibilities, leaving ourselves and others even more stressed, or 2) our Micro-Retreat will not be sustainable.

Gathering Support

Your spouse, kid(s), work, or friend needs you. I get that. I am married and have three young kids under five. As I'm writing this, my wife is pregnant with our fourth. Life is busy!

Still, my wife and I have a relationship where we understand this practice is important for both of us. To accommodate it, we each take an early morning on the weekend. Either she or I will take Saturday morning or Sunday morning, respectively. It means we usually don't do social events on Saturday or Sunday mornings. Despite the other things we've said no to, these times have proven to be transformative rhythms for us individually and together as a family.

Step 4: Plan how you want to spend your time.

When I go on a date with my wife, I will sometimes jot down the things I want to share with her. They could be a parenting challenge we're having, something I wanted to encourage her with, or even some conflict in our lives. Of course, any structure we set is flexible. Yet I find that coming prepared with a conversation list allows our dates to be rich and meaningful.

I have found that this approach to Micro-Retreats is also helpful. We don't want to be accomplishment-oriented or miss out on organic moments. Yet I find it helpful, at the start of this time, to write down a list of things I want to talk to God about. It may be marriage, parenting, work, dreams, or a feeling I haven't had time to process.

Before you go, spend a few minutes jotting down some ideas so the time you spend can nourish your soul in the way you need.

Step 5: When you arrive, unplug from devices.

I ensure that any time with digital devices is wholly planned and extremely limited (looking for directions, checking in with home at set hours). It may mean turning your phone off and dropping it in the bottom of your bag. Or it could mean downloading your music ahead of time and putting your phone on airplane mode. If you're actively messaging someone, let them know you'll have to log out for a bit. If it's safe for you to leave your devices altogether, do it. The less you bring, the more you can be engaged.

Step 6: Decompress.

To fully engage in the practices, we need time to decompress. Most of us will enter this time with a week full of stress, worry, and anxiety. They will be centered in our minds, and we'll struggle to engage.

In therapy, I learned to do something called "Morning Pages." It's a time to brain dump and write a stream of consciousness. In the Micro-Retreat, I think back on the week and write what comes to mind. Once it is out of my mind and onto the page, I feel ready to engage. I have validated the stream of thoughts by giving them a home on my page, and I can release them from my mind knowing I can come back to find them there if needed.

Step 7: Spend quality time with God.

This step is the meat of this practice. We've made all the preparations, now is the time to enjoy the date. Bring up the questions you prepared and flip to one of the practices in this book. Plan to spend a lot of time reflecting, journaling, and praying. You may also integrate things like walking, reading, or doing art. It's *your* time with God—spend it how you feel most connected to each other.

Every week calls for something different. I try to take inventory of my heart and soul to determine what I need. Use the other practices in this book as a resource.

Here are my go-to practices:

- Practice 4: Intentional Silence (To nourish my soul with God's voice amid all of life's noises)
- Practice 5: Personal Reflection (To help me understand what happened in my crazy week)
- Practice 6: Listening Prayer (Because I want to see from his perspective)
- Practice 9: Identity Meditation (Because insecurity is often a side effect of a chaotic life)

Step 8: Return well.

Micro-Retreats are not just to give you peace and connection that evaporates into thin air the second you step back into the world. They recharge you and change you as a person as you engage with the world around you.

As you near the end of your time, you may spend a few minutes thinking about the week ahead. What challenges do you anticipate? Is there anything you want to do differently this week? What truths from your time retreating do you want to permeate the week ahead? Try to go slow for the rest of the day, if you can, and tell someone else what you were hearing or processing during your time.

Note: See the practices in "Returning" for more ideas on returning well.

Leaning into Joy

Here's one final thought I want to leave with you. Micro-Retreats are for you and God to enjoy one another. As someone who's a high producer, it can be tempting to say, "I want to do x, y, z in this time." And many times, I do get to talk to God about those things. But what has helped is really relaxing my approach to Micro-Retreats. It is first about decompressing and letting God lead me.

Micro-Retreats are not work. Find locations that give you joy. I enjoy a good coffee, so the first hour of my Micro-Retreat is sitting at a coffee shop and journaling and reflecting with my headphones on. It's life-giving for me.

What's life-giving for you? If it's walking in the park, enjoying the scenery, or grabbing a snack, do those things. Do restorative things. Just make sure to be talking with God as you do it. Come back a better and more alive person.

A Micro-Retreat is an incredibly effective time for modern Christians to withdraw from our contexts. It is a rhythm that makes space to explore various practices, working multiple "spiritual muscles" at once. Use it as a weekly sharpener of your spiritual life so that you are ready to tackle the chaos of the following week with God.

PRACTICE 3

Personal Retreat:
The Seasonal Realignment

*Our patterns of work and rest reveal what we believe to be true
about God and ourselves. God alone requires no limits on his
activity. To rest is to acknowledge that we humans are limited
by design. We are created for rest just as surely as we are
created for labor. An inability or unwillingness to cease from
our labors is a confession of unbelief, an admission that we
view ourselves as creator and sustainer of our own universes.*

JEN WILKIN

O n this particular retreat, I felt led to talk with God about one of
the most painful seasons of my life and how to pick up the pieces
from the aftermath.

Ten years prior, I left seminary early and entered therapy to work
on unresolved issues that stemmed from my childhood. After this
season of healing, I became a better man. Still, I ended up on a different
path than when I first started seminary.

I didn't go into full-time ministry or become a pastor. I entered a "normal" job, and, while I continued serving in my church, I didn't leave seminary doing what I expected I'd be doing. Mostly, I ignored this discontentment and tried to have a good attitude.

Ten years later, I couldn't help but struggle with deep disappointment. Though you couldn't see it on my face, I carried a deeply planted sense of shame and failure. Like shadows, they followed me everywhere in life. Due to my busy life, I never had the time to address it. There was always something to do, some responsibility that needed my attention.

As much as I'd tried to ignore them, these feelings stirred up again as I anticipated my upcoming Personal Retreat. I was able to avoid it for a long time, but I sensed that God was discontent with these feelings living deep within my heart. This abysmal wound was still having an enormous impact on my life. And I knew this retreat was when God and I would have the time to talk about it.

On this sunny spring day, I sat on an old wooden bench at this retreat center. "Okay, God, if this is what you want to talk about, what do you want to say?"

The next few hours would turn out to be the most transformative hours of my life. It was like a light bulb turned on in my heart. I began to see a different perspective I'd never thought of before. I felt like God was saying, "I'm proud of you, son," even in an area of my life where I only saw failure. I could now see how God was moving during that time.

Slowly, I picked up my pen and wrote the words "formative desert." This phrase represented that while the season was tough, I now saw it as a desert God specifically used to form me in unique ways. That transformation was not lost on me. God was using it as part of a redemptive arc that I could never have imagined alone. It was good news.

I took a deep breath, nodded slowly, and uttered a prayer of thanksgiving under my breath. I walked away that morning with a new smile—the smile of a changed man.

We can often assume that Personal Retreats are only for the clergy. As someone who wasn't in vocational ministry, taking a few days just for myself felt impractical and selfish. While I gave my retreat-taking leaders a big thumbs up, I hadn't thought of a Personal Retreat as something I could or should do myself. I assumed it was easy for them to schedule, focus, sit still, and to hear God because they were ministers. Not "regular people" like me.

Over time, however, I began to realize: God's calling for regular people is every bit as important as God's calling for people in vocational ministry. Even though I wasn't working at a church, I understood my calling to work, to be a husband, a father, and a witness was just as meaningful. God ordained that calling in those contexts and others. And because they were important, I needed to be locked in spiritually so I could be faithful to everything God gave me.

If you have a calling on your life (yes, you do) and struggle with a busy, chaotic life (I bet you do), then I believe taking Personal Retreats can strongly aid in your ability to live it out. What is a Personal Retreat?

> A Personal Retreat is a set of days where we leave our usual context to be still, be in God's presence, and dive deep within ourselves with the hope of great spiritual transformation.

I try to practice this at least once a year. It helps set long-term vision and clarity in ways that a daily walk or Micro-Retreat cannot do. Many of my most profound and highest revelations from God have happened in the context of retreats. I still remember the deep and lasting words I received during those times.

The Power of the Personal Retreat

Why do Personal Retreats have such a strong impact compared to smaller retreats we can do daily or weekly?

1. Personal Retreats multiply the depth we can access with God.

While this practice is similar to the Micro-Retreat, the two differ in that the Personal Retreat allows us to go even deeper, and it requires some extra preparations. In our daily lives, even in Micro-Retreats, we're stealing moments with God. However, the Personal Retreat is when we get to spend all day together. It's like being on vacation with someone we love.

Removed from the force of urgency, we can wander through areas of our lives, hearts, and minds that have been placed on the backburner: hidden wounds, deep questions, and seedling dreams. When we are dealing with issues of the soul, things take time to surface. We cannot achieve this level of reflection and refreshment in the crush of everyday life.

Removed from the force of urgency, we can wander through areas of our lives, hearts, and minds that have been placed on the backburner: hidden wounds, deep questions, and seedling dreams.

2. The increased buy-in of retreats helps us receive more.

Personal Retreats are not easy for many reasons. Since they span a couple of days, you will likely have to pay to stay. Or if you go further away, you must arrange travel plans. Many may see this as a negative or hindrance. But this is a key part of the retreat's power.

Would you be more likely to work out if you paid for an expensive gym membership? Would you be more likely to attend a class if you had to turn down another opportunity for it? Probably. We are more likely to follow through and take something seriously when we have buy-in. The buy-in required for this kind of retreat helps us focus and engage in the time we spend.

3. Personal Retreats allow us to be nurtured by a new environment.

In the Micro-Retreat, if we only have a couple of hours, we probably don't want to spend half our time driving, so we're limited in how far we can go. But in Personal Retreats, we have the space to go farther into new environments that nurture us.

When I suggest locations for people to go for Personal Retreats, I almost always recommend finding dedicated retreat properties. In nearly every metropolis area, you can find enclaves of buildings and retreat centers across different denominations. Often, these centers are hosted by denominations that focus more on the contemplative practices of Christianity. That may feel jarring for those whose spiritual "comfort food" consists of busy, charismatic gatherings and loud, boisterous worship like mine. However, I am constantly amazed and humbled when I experience the quiet magnitude of other traditions that make space at these centers.

These places are committed to helping people engage with God. When I went to a Franciscan Monastery in Malibu, built to host retreats, everything on campus was engineered for my spiritual transformation. They provided the meals, a beautiful garden in which to walk and pray, and a prayer chapel. They even had the stations of the cross outside for me to kneel and reflect. All of this was designed to calm my brain, eliminate distractions, and remove every barrier to God's presence.

Whether we attend a retreat center, an Airbnb, a hotel, or a friend's backhouse, this expanded retreat allows us to access locations designed for our restoration. It multiplies our ability to be fully present and hungry for God's voice.

How to Practice the Personal Retreat

Step 1: Schedule your block of time.

If your life can afford it, try taking two to four days away. However, I know many of you can't take a vacation. Maybe you don't have paid time off, you can't get childcare, you have weekly commitments, or project deadlines weigh on your shoulders. For those who can't afford to take two or four days away, a two-day retreat on a weekend is a perfect window. At a minimum, a two-day, one-night stay somewhere can provide immense depth and restoration.

Schedule your next Personal Retreat ahead of time, and protect it as you'd protect a commitment to a conference or a family vacation. It's a sacrifice, but I want to encourage you that this is almost always attainable for working people with busy lives if we plan and align our priorities. Do not feel guilty about telling people you're unavailable during that time.

Step 2: Research and choose your location.

While location preference is subjective, a good rule of thumb is to go at least a two-hour drive away. Pick a location that will contribute to the restoration of your soul. Choose somewhere near the ocean or a forest. Cozy up in a lazy little town.

Of course, you can find a serene hotel, Airbnb, or backhouse. Or, as I mentioned, look into monasteries or retreat centers. If you search on the internet for one near you, you will most likely find quite a few. Most of them will offer overnights or day trips where you can stay at a hotel nearby. Some will even have guided options where a trained chaplain, priest, or pastor can give you a framework to engage with your time. These locations will be highly conducive to your retreats.

Step 3: Find a spiritual guide.

Often, I consult a spiritual guide or mentor figure before a retreat to point out what I might need at that time. It usually involves someone I respect at church. I say, "I'm going on a Personal Retreat. Can you discern what I should be doing with my time? What questions do I need to ask?"

If they know me well, they can see into my blind spots and challenge me toward the dreams I have. Even if they don't know me, they can share with me what they're sensing from God and give me creative ideas. This also brings a form of accountability—you may feel more inclined to ask yourself the hard questions when you know someone will be following up afterward. It also may be less daunting to know you can process what comes up with a spiritual leader upon your return.

Many times, the retreat centers will have their own spiritual guides. Depending on whether you're comfortable with their spiritual and theological approach, that might work well for you. Whoever you choose, I encourage you to involve the wisdom and discernment of your faith community.

Step 4: Make a list of practices you want to do on retreat.

A Personal Retreat creates much more space to fill. That can be freeing, or it may feel daunting. What I've found helpful is that when I'm on a retreat, typically, I plan a list of practices to do. I recommend flipping through this book and picking out a practice or two for each day.

Step 5: Make a rough schedule of your retreat.

I'll jot down a rough schedule on a piece of paper. Granted, it's not a strict plan, but a guide is helpful to make sure I can cover what's most important.

Here is a rough example of what you might see in my plan:

7 a.m.	Wake up
7:30 a.m.	Worship + Reading of Psalms + Thanksgiving
8:30–9 a.m.	Breakfast
9–11 a.m.	Reflect on Marriage
11–11:30 a.m.	Walk and Intercede for Marriage
12 p.m.	Lunch
1:00 p.m.	Nap
2–4 p.m.	Reflect on Calling
4–4:30 p.m.	Walk and Pray for Calling
5:00 p.m.	Dinner
6–6:30 p.m.	Silence in Nature
6:30–8 p.m.	Reflect on Work

Faithfulness Map

A powerful exercise I do in my Personal Retreats is what I call the "faithfulness map." I write down all the categories in my life, e.g., work, marriage, parenting, ministry, etc. I spend extended time reflecting on each category with God. The kind of reflection I do in the faithfulness map is to assess how faithful I am in each of these areas of my life.

One of the most important questions I ask when reflecting upon my life is, "What do you think, God?" I will sit quietly and listen to what his Spirit says to me. Many times, I will have an insight I didn't see before about my work, marriage, parenting, etc.

From this map, I will prayerfully consider, "What's my next step?" I force myself to ask the question, "How can I be faithful in this area of my life?" This exercise allows me to appraise every area God has entrusted to me.

Step 6: Consolidate your resolutions and make them visible.

We know from scripture that God loves to communicate with and lead us. It's likely that you will come back with new insights, reflections, and revelations. You may find that you want to do some things differently as you go forward.

It is wise to consolidate the list of things you want to do coming home from your retreat. Consider hanging that list on a wall so it's in your view at home.

Step 7: Share with the community.

In my retreat journal, I make notes of revelations, insights, or reflections that I want to share with particular people.

The first person I share with is always my wife. She is my life partner life. And more than likely, she would have been busy watching the kids so I could go. She will want to know what her sacrifice produced! But sharing the things I reflect on from my retreat is one of the treasures we can use in marriage. Most married people long for a deep connection with their spouses. Everything I share with my wife from my retreat draws us closer together. For those who are married, I encourage you to schedule time to share some salient highlights from your time alone with God.

For all of you, married or not, I recommend scheduling time to share with your faith community. If you are being spiritually mentored by someone, share the things that God spoke to you for their assessment and encouragement. For those of you in small groups or life groups, consider sharing the things God spoke to you as a blessing to your community. Share with your roommates. Who knows? It might encourage them to go on retreat as well.

Gift a Personal Retreat

One of the things my wife and I do in our marriage is gift each other Personal Retreats. Sure, we get each other massages and other gifts, but because I love my wife, I want her to be her best self. Knowing my wife and the types of trips she enjoys, I have surprised her with tickets and time to make a retreat. She has historically come back changed and refreshed. Consider making this a habit to strengthen your marriage.

The Personal Retreat is a powerful tool in a Christian's toolbelt. While it requires some sacrifice, the longevity of this practice allows a unique level of breadth, depth, reflection, and healing. Ultimately, the retreat helps realign us with the big-picture vision God has for our lives.

Learning to Be Still

The faster life is, the slower I need to go.
JOHN LO

But they who wait for the Lord shall renew their strength;
they shall mount up with wings like eagles; they shall
run and not be weary; they shall walk and not faint.
ISAIAH 40

I finished my workday, started making dinner, fed the kids, cleaned up the house for our guests, and then welcomed everyone as they arrived. They were also reaching the end of busy days and weeks. As they began slowing down and settling into couches and chairs around the wide wooden table, I continued my forward motion by serving food and trying to get our girls into bed. Yet I was interrupted by a question.

"So, Phil, what did you do this week?"

I continued scooping pasta for a moment as my brain hardly registered that my guest was talking to me. I looked up at her with the tongs still moving in my hand. It was a simple question to include me in the conversation, but I fumbled for an answer.

She continued looking at me, waiting for my response.

After a moment of sifting through my brain fog, I couldn't come up with anything. "To be honest, I can barely remember. I've just been going nonstop."

She gave me a knowing nod, and nobody thought it was peculiar that I couldn't answer her question. They understood the feeling.

Have you ever ended a day wondering to yourself, "Where did the day go? What happened today?" Perhaps a glaze comes over your eyes, in a state of busy-induced amnesia. *What happened? What did I do? Was what I did important?*

It happens to me all the time. And I hate it. It feels as if I am in one of those new self-driving cars. At some point, I stopped driving and slipped into autopilot, but the car kept moving. Now, I place my hands back on the wheel to regain control, but I have already traveled without knowing where I was going or if I wanted to go there. By the time I come back to my senses, I don't even know where I am.

I hate this feeling because I know it means I lived absently. As I reflect on the week, I wonder how often I accidentally ignored my wife or brushed off one of my daughters attempting to get my attention because I was focused on staying in motion with the next task in front of me. I imagine how many strangers I walked by briskly who could have used a hand or a kind word. Under the guise of focus, I lived inattentively. I did it again. It's maddening.

It may be funny and lighthearted to say, "Where did today go?" But when this feeling becomes a constant over weeks, months, even years, I know I have a bigger problem: in trying to make the most of my life, I've gone so fast that I wasted it.

Do we think God intended for us to live purposeless lives? Or for us to live blindly from one life event to another? Of course not! God created us to be alive, purposeful, and fruitful. We are to be present in God-given moments. Even beyond that, God intends for us to see the heavenly realities occurring around us. Beyond being able to say what I did this week, I also want to be able to see what *God* did all around me.

Yet over and over in my life, especially when things are crazy, life moves me at breakneck speeds. This autopilot happens to me. My calendar events look like they're in bumper-to-bumper traffic, one after another. I am in the passenger seat at the mercy of where they take me. It is as if someone or something coerced me into a ride I didn't agree to, even as I continued to consent. Perhaps you feel this same frustration, this same angst.

What do we do?

I remember something my pastor said to me that I hadn't understood until now. One time, we were planning an event together. The event date was nearing, and we hadn't prepared as much as I felt we should have because it had been so difficult to coordinate our schedules for a simple phone call. I was running around errand to errand even as we finally started our call. I clamped the phone between my shoulder and ear, frantically asking what was needed.

> My calendar events look like they're in bumper-to-bumper traffic, one after another. I am in the passenger seat at the mercy of where they take me. It is as if someone or something coerced me into a ride I didn't agree to, even as I continued to consent.

My shaky, urgent tone was countered with his voice, calm and steady. He could tell I was in a frenetic zone. Unrushed and level-headed, he could see above the urgency to a greater momentary need. He didn't speed up in the middle of our conversation about logistics. Recognizing a moment of teaching, he paused.

He calmly said, "Phil, I have found that the faster life goes, the slower I need to go."

Waiting at a stop light, I tapped my fingers on the steering wheel, waiting for him to be done with his sage wisdom so we could get back to planning.

Aloud, I probably thanked him through clenched teeth.

That sounds novel. I have no idea what it means.
Maybe one day I'll understand.

The Day Jesus Slowed Down

Read: John 11:1–16

It wasn't until I observed the life of Jesus that I understood the wisdom of slowing to a halt.

As we've mentioned before, Jesus's life held an enormous amount of pressure. And he didn't have the latest project management app or the newest self-help book about how to do more in less time. However, the story of Lazarus reveals the second major chaos-countering rhythm in Jesus' life: being still.

The story starts with Jesus ministering in a town quite far from where siblings Mary, Martha, and Lazarus lived. They were three of Jesus's closest friends. Jesus sat at their table for hours, eating, talking, and laughing together. They *knew* Jesus. They trusted him and believed he loved them.

When Lazarus fell ill, there was nothing more his sisters could do to help him. Their only hope for Lazarus' survival was for Jesus to come and intervene immediately. They fully believed in Jesus's ability to heal their brother, if only he could get there in time.

They sent a messenger who walked for days to try and get to Jesus in time. When the messenger finally reached Jesus, the man was likely out of breath, his muscles aching from hurrying. Someone's life was on the line! There's no doubt he and everyone else expected Jesus to leave at that moment—run to rescue his friend.

In this time pressure, Jesus did something ludicrous. It says in John 11:5 that instead of immediately rushing to help, he stayed two more days in the place where he was. Two days! What was he thinking? Why didn't he go immediately? Maybe he was in denial about Lazarus' actual condition. Perhaps he didn't care about Lazarus at all. I can only imagine the mixture of sorrow, confusion, anger, and defeat running through the messenger's mind. His steps must have dragged through the dirt as he walked back, knowing Lazarus wouldn't make it.

Rather than moving at a pace to meet the genuine pressures of the world's call to him, Jesus stays still a bit longer.

Finally, Jesus went to Lazarus. It took a couple more days to reach his friends' house. But he arrived to the news that Lazarus had already died. He was too late.

People were disappointed in him. They were filled with grief and frustration over the death and the fact that their healer lost his race against the clock. With unveiled emotion, Martha told Jesus in John 11:21, "If you were here, my brother wouldn't have died." And the scripture says Jesus wept. Not that he was misty-eyed—he *wept*.

People probably thought Jesus was crying because he knew he was too late, but that was not the case. Jesus then asked to be led to Lazarus' tomb. At this point, Lazarus had been dead for four days. Jesus rolls aside the stone covering his tomb and calls Lazarus to come out. To everyone's amazement, Lazarus does. The dead man walked out of his grave.

In this pre-story, we see that Jesus did not lose the race against the clock, was not too late, and did not run out of time. Instead, we see that Jesus responded to the pressure to hurry by doing the exact opposite. Rather than running out of time, Jesus defies the power of time as we know it.

What happened to Jesus that day happens to all of us. It is the voice of hurry beckoning. There are many reasons to move and to keep moving. Maybe you experience your kids yelling at you. Your boss. Your work schedule. In this instance, a real-world need pressured Jesus to respond. He did something that we, in our haste, struggle or flat-out refuse to do. *He stayed still.* Jesus's decision was not made out of denial, carelessness, or lack of love; it was an act of wisdom and intentionality.

> Stillness is an intentional time when we resist the world's pressure to move and wait for God's direction.

This story shows us that there are times to stand against the common assumptions about time and action. There are times to stop, slow down, and make sure we are in sync with God. We must question the idea that the demands placed on us and those we place on ourselves must always take priority.

We often hate slowing down because we think it's counterproductive. From Jesus's example, slowing down can also be interpreted as neglectful and uncaring. We may struggle to say no to commitments for this very same reason—after all, why wouldn't you want to lead another church group, help your friend move, or take on more at work to help your coworker out? Yet the truth is that a life lived slower is a life that accomplishes more.

How Stillness Creates Resilience

When we allow ourselves to slow down enough to savor the gift of total stillness, we begin to see the superpower it holds.

1. Stillness declares that the clock is not our god.

In our culture, time is undoubtedly one of our most prized resources. I don't know about you, but I'm quicker to give my money to a cause than I am to give my time. My time is so precious to me and feels so scarce. New apps and businesses and kiosks open daily, all oriented around time-saving and time management. There are countless self-help books devoted to making us more efficient—in other words, helping us accomplish more in the same amount of time. It's common to hear phrases like "I don't have time" or "There aren't enough hours in the day." This idea of time as a precious yet stringent force is well-known in our culture.

The clock often rules our daily lives. Rather than asking God what we should do in a day, we check how much time we have open. Rather than asking God if we should stop to talk with someone, we ask our clock, and it says we're running late. The clock tells us when to get up and reprimands us when we've gotten up too late. An exacting ruler, the clock produces massive anxiety in our lives, and we accept it, often without question.

When we live like this, we implicitly assume that time is an objective reality higher than God's. Like Mary, Martha, and the others, we assume time constrains Jesus like it does us. In this assumption, we make God smaller, and we make the clock our master.

Stillness declares that we live by what God says rather than solely by the clock. Stillness is an act of trust that God's reality is higher than our own. All throughout scripture, God gives people missions that do not adhere to what should be possible in our human understanding of the world. Stillness is simply another example of this, defying the human constraints of time to put God back in his rightful place.

2. Stillness allows us to see what we've missed.

Imagine you are on the freeway. Going over sixty miles per hour, what do you see of your surroundings? If you're in LA like me, you see tall buildings whizzing by, an occasional tree, and the mountains far off in the distance. If you're driving through a neighborhood, going maybe twenty miles per hour, you see individual houses and can read street signs and billboards. When you walk through the neighborhood, you notice the neighbor's yard sign, a wild burst of colorful flowers, and your partner's voice beside you. When you are absolutely still, you see the most—the ripples in the tree bark from the fire five years ago, a quiet whisper of the Holy Spirit in your ear. In stillness, we discover a whole new world.

I am repeatedly reminded that I don't realize how much I don't see until I finally stop and look—both in the external and my inner world. In our minds and hearts, we zip by a conversation or a surprising emotion so fast we can't process it. How can we understand what happened or what it can teach us? The difference is enormous, and if we never sit still, we will miss vital observations and insights that would otherwise recenter and shape us.

3. Stillness allows us to live purposefully.

Do you know that feeling when you are running down a hill, and you can't stop? Your right foot pounds down right after your left. There is no time to plan where you're stepping. The force of your momentum propels you forward. All you can do to keep yourself from falling on your face is to keep running.

This is similar to what happens in our frenetic lives. The momentum of our day-to-day busyness builds until all we can do is keep running or fall flat on our faces. Most people live their whole lives this way, only crawling to a stop when they physically cannot keep going. It is most often at the end of one's life when people sit up in their beds and realize the haunting truth: "I have lived my life poorly." It's in slowness that they can distinguish the unimportant from the important.

To live purposefully, we must be in spaces where life's pace does not obfuscate the invaluable from the worthless. When we take time out of our busy lives, we enter a state where we can assess what's important or unimportant. This is crucial if we want to live lives of meaning, significance, and faithfulness.

Three Practices for Stillness

Stillness is where we follow Jesus's example in trusting God with our time. We slow down enough to see what's going on in and around us, and pivot to pursue what's most important. In the next chapters, I will present three practices to make stillness a regular rhythm in our lives.

Practice 4: Intentional Silence

Practice 5: Personal Reflection

Practice 6: Listening Prayer

Intentional Silence: Being Fully Present in a Noisy World

A talkative soul lacks both the essential virtues and intimacy with God. A deeper interior life, one of gentle peace and of that silence where the Lord dwells, is quite out of the question. A soul that has never tasted the sweetness of inner silence is a restless spirit which disturbs the silence of others.

ST. FAUSTINA

God speaks in the silence of the heart.
Listening is the beginning of prayer.

MOTHER TERESA

My wife Esther and I have a date night just about every week. The best dates with my wife have one element in common: long, deep, meaningful conversations. During those times, I genuinely feel connected to her. The intimacy we create is based on the fact that we understand each other and we feel understood. But our conversations weren't always as rich and fruitful as they are now.

Earlier in our marriage, I talked a lot more on our dates. I wanted Esther to know every thought in my head, all the dreams in my heart, and everything that happened to me that day. But as time passed, she pointed out that the more I talked, the less I listened to her. *Duh.* Sometimes I was busy thinking about what I wanted to say next rather than taking in what she shared with me, and she could tell. I wanted to listen better. I wanted to hear her heart's thoughts, feelings, and dreams.

This obvious concept clicked for me in a new way: when one person shares, the other listens. It is not listening if I'm trying to interject, talk over her, or if I'm on my phone. Listening is not a passive exercise but one full of attentiveness.

This may seem apparent to most, but I realized that to listen, one must be silent. Silence needed to become my friend if I was to become a better listener. Therein lies a secret truth about silence: Silence is not just the absence of noise—Intentional Silence is the exercise of listening. Like the deep conversations I can have with my wife, silence is about being able to hear well.

> Intentional Silence is the practice of listening intently to God and our own soul amid the world's many noises.

I yearned for a deep spirituality for so long but didn't know how to obtain it. As this understanding about silence with my wife began to click, I felt challenged to grow my intimacy with God the way I was growing it with my wife. I started treating our time together like a two-way street and not dominating the conversations as I leaned in to hear God speak.

Silence is not a prominent value in our American culture. We tend to value the outspoken and the boisterous, even in Christian circles. We tend to see the loud as the leaders and overlook the silent as passive. Yet as I began regularly making space for Intentional Silence in my life, I felt convicted by how far this is from the way scripture describes our noise.

My soul, be quiet before God,
for from him comes my hope.
Psalm 62:5

There is a time to tear and a time to sew;
a time to be silent and a time to speak.
Ecclesiastes 3:7

Stand in silence in the presence of the Sovereign LORD.
Zephaniah 1:7

The Lord is in His holy temple, let all the
earth keep silence before Him.
Habakkuk 2:20

I began to realize silence is the gift that modern Christians need. Every sound, sight, voice, and ping pulls us in a different direction. We struggle to feel "present." We live disembodied lives, in an inauthentic state of ourselves, disconnected from God. We don't even know what state we're in, especially in a crisis, when a thousand voices pull us further and further from our authentic selves.

Intentional Silence is still challenging for me, bringing up many of the same struggles as stillness. As a lover of constant noise, even in the background, my thoughts swarm in the absence of stimuli, like I am poking a beehive that a steady stream of noise has quelled. Yet as I stubbornly continue to practice it, silence is also now something that grounds me. I have come to realize that silence is a friend that helps me hear myself, others, and God more clearly.

The Power of Intentional Silence

Three critical components make Intentional Silence an effective tool for building resilience.

1. Silence fosters our attentiveness.

Many of us face constant voices around us. Whether it is the voice of our boss, our spouse, our church members, or even our kids, we are besieged. When too many voices surround us, it's hard to fully pay attention to any single one, let alone discern the most important one. Silence helps us focus in on one voice at a time.

2. Silence allows us to hear our soul.

How common is the sight at a bus stop, waiting room, or even standing in line at a department store, where everyone is on their phone? Maybe the room is silent, but everyone has earbuds, taking in noise. We are so accustomed to being connected that it is *strange* to find someone sitting on a bench doing nothing. The irony of being connected to everyone and everything is that we have no awareness of our own internal state.

In Intentional Silence, our soul makes itself known. If we turn down the noise, we can hear what it is trying to say. We can listen to its pains. We can hear its joys, and we can hear what it needs. And hearing the state of our soul is the first step in healing it. As the disparate parts of our lives come back together, our souls start their journey of becoming healthier.

3. Silence allows us to hear the whisper of God.

One of my favorite things about Intentional Silence is that it provides the exact conditions where I am open to hearing God's voice. The adage is true: it is not that God is not speaking; it is that we are not listening.

Listening requires my ears not to be occupied by anything else. God is not willing to compete with the noise that surrounds us.

In silence, my prayers are more potent and hit closer to home. Instead of vague prayers for help, I learn what my soul needs so I can ask precisely.

> The adage is true: it is not that God is not speaking; it is that we are not listening. Listening requires my ears not to be occupied by anything else. God is not willing to compete with the noise that surrounds us.

Ultimately, silence provides a beautiful space where we simultaneously listen to ourselves and God.

How to Practice Intentional Silence

Step 1: Schedule times of silence.

When do you want to practice this? When do you feel like your soul needs it most? You may need a few minutes of silence at the end of a long day in your car before you go inside. You might need it right before work to start with a state of calm. You can integrate it into your weekly Micro-Retreat or Prayer Walk. Think of a moment when you need a bit of silence in your life and write it down.

Step 2: Unplug from all digital noise.

During your time of silence, put your phone on airplane mode or turn it off completely. The bing or buzz of our devices immediately draws our attention from listening. Some people practice digital detoxing, periods where we are far away from anything digital for extended blocks of time. It's important to silence digital noise while we practice silence, even if it's only for a few minutes.

Step 3: Set a timer.

If you're not used to sitting in silence, one minute can feel like an hour. You can take a less structured approach to silence by gazing at nature, sitting still, or going on a walk. But if it's helpful for you to take a more structured approach, start small and set a timer when beginning. Try one minute. Try two. Five. Ten. Allow your mind to get used to it, like exercising a muscle.

Step 4: Use breath prayers.

Silence is about being fully connected with ourselves so we can be fully connected with God. Our physical bodies can help us with this. Breathing is a powerful way of connectedness and being present. Author and spiritual director Bill Gaultiere says, "Breathing a prayer to God is a simple way of using your body to engage your mind on the Word of God. Whispering the words of scripture as you are breathing in and out, slowly and deeply, over and over, can help you to 'abide' in Christ (John 15:4,5,9)." Spend a few minutes just breathing, imagining God's presence flowing through you.

> ### Ideas to Anchor Your Attention in Silence
>
> In a small group with my pastor, he would often start the meetings by asking, "How is your soul?" It was a question of reflection and introspection. Prompts like this ask the more intimate things going on in our hearts, minds, and souls. Here are some prompts to anchor our minds in silence:
>
> - Soul, how are you emotionally?
> - How is your hope level?

- Are you carrying pain?
- How is your strength?
- Think of a scripture and repeat it in your mind.
- Picture the face of Jesus; what do you see?
- Observe the world around you, studying the details of your environment.

Step 5: Invite the Holy Spirit as a friend in silence.

I invite the Holy Spirit whenever I practice Intentional Silence. When we engage in silence alone, it is frightening to sometimes face the pains in our souls. But the Holy Spirit is a comforter (2 Corinthians 1), a friend (John 14:26), and a counselor (John 14:16).

I imagine God's presence is with me on the bench. And as I'm listening to my soul, I occasionally pray about the things I see and hear. I observe what is happening in my soul and ask him, "What do you think about that, God?" These questions have led to rich and intimate conversations. There have been many times in silence when I have needed the Holy Spirit's strength, guidance, and healing voice to guide me through painful confrontations in my heart.

Silence as a Trigger

Silence can bring up very uncomfortable emotions for me. When we take time to listen, we may hear past pains and hurts. And that can be very intimidating. For many, silence is a strong trigger for past trauma. It can prompt extreme anxiety or even a panic attack. If you've experienced this, please know you are no less faithful or close to God because of challenges from your past.

If you relate to this concern, you may want to talk to a counselor or therapist—someone trained to help you address past trauma. These experiences can overwhelm us, and I don't want to underestimate their impact on our ability to commune with God. To read more about trauma's impact on how we experience spiritual practices, I recommend reading *Trauma in the Pews: The Impact on Faith and Spiritual Practices* by Dr. Janyne McConnaughey.

To thrive in our crazy, overly connected, chaotic times, we must have rhythms of silence in our lives. Constant noise is the catalyst for fragmentation and disconnection. Intentional Silence is the secret to being present and connected.

Personal Reflection: Reclaiming Vision in the Whirlwind

If today were your last, would you do what you're doing?
MAX LUCADO

Journaling is like whispering to one's self
and listening at the same time.
MINA MURRAY, DRACULA

W hen I was in seminary, I took a spiritual and organizational leadership class from Professor Scott Cormode. I was used to the typical lecture format: the professor talks for the entire class period, and I sit and take notes. But Scott's class was not like this.

Rather than the typical format, Scott would often lecture for about half of the class. For the second half, he would break the students into groups, and we would sit there and talk about what we were learning for the rest of our time. We'd answer questions about the lecture, break it down into its components, see how it related to other things we'd learned, and talk about how it could be applied. Occasionally, I could recognize the value of this time, but usually, it felt like we were repeating the lecture rather than learning something new.

It annoyed me at first. After all, I wasn't spending all this tuition money to talk to my classmates! In my view, this class format cut my overall learning in half. I felt like I was getting skimped. He didn't explain why he did this. Yet by the end of the class, something surprised me.

Out of all the classes I'd taken that semester, I realized that I learned the most in this class. In other classes, we covered more material, but I only remembered maybe a quarter of it. But for Scott's class, I remembered almost everything I learned. What's more, in his class, I left with a much better understanding of how to apply the material in a variety of circumstances. I was much more comfortable explaining it to others because it was ingrained in my brain.

Finally, at the end of the semester, Scott gave us an explanation. Quoting American philosopher John Dewey, he said, "We do not learn from experience. We learn from *reflecting* on experience." Taking this seriously, Scott built reflection into the very infrastructure of our class so we would not only hear and take in the content but *learn* it.

I now understand this principle for the class setting and the rest of our lives. We commonly say, "Experience is the best teacher," but experience is no teacher at all. It's evidenced by seeing people in our lives making the same mistakes repeatedly. We can find ourselves in this cycle of never-learning too. It resonates with the famous quote from Socrates that claims, "The unexamined life is not worth living." Having an experience without reflecting on it is like taking a class but not learning anything—somewhat pointless. It does not move us forward in any way.

When we reflect, we give meaning to our experiences. We take a posture of curiosity rather than taking things at face value and making snap assumptions. Whatever our initial interpretation is, we gain more clarity and insight in the time we spend thinking, processing, rehashing, and analyzing the narrative we believe. That requires an intentional choice to engage in examination, and that process takes time.

Personal Reflection is a critical tool that allows us to see through the craziness and become resilient amid chaos. What exactly is it?

> Personal Reflection is the practice of prayerfully looking back at events, thoughts, feelings, or actions to gain new understanding and inform faithful next steps.

Personal Reflection is an active exercise of thinking about life. It takes a posture of curiosity. It's time to ask questions, wonder, pray, and understand; it involves analytical thinking about what's going on.

While the Bible uses different language to describe it, there are many places where God commands reflection. One example is Haggai 1:5, where God tells the Israelites, "Consider your ways. You have sown much and harvested little. You eat, but you never have enough; you drink, but you never have your fill." In this passage, the people are enjoying the fruits of returning from exile. They are busy working, harvesting, and sowing. But they are so busy that they have missed what's important—rebuilding the temple and seeking their God.

God points out this problem, charging them to stop and look at it for what it is. The key word God uses to indicate reflection is "consider." Stop harvesting. Stop sowing. Stop building. Stop what you are doing and *think carefully about this.*

I resonate with the Israelites here. I used to think that reflecting was a waste of time. "Who has time to just sit there and think?" I would say to myself. "I have too many things to do and tasks to accomplish and meetings to attend to set aside precious time to sit and ponder. I'll leave that for the monks." I trudged on in life, believing that action was better than contemplation.

My resistance to reflecting came from several sources. For one, I don't like being bored. Living a life of extreme busyness gives us the sense that we're doing something important when we might not be doing anything that needs to be done. Reflecting meant cutting myself off from this stimulation and calming my brain down. I equated calmness with boredom.

On a deeper level, the stillness required for Personal Reflection can trigger stronger emotions in us than we might want to confront. Continuous motion was all I could do in many seasons to keep from breaking down. Perhaps depression, anxiety, disappointment, or fears crouch at the door, waiting for a moment of free space in your brain to take over completely. It's a prevalent response to trauma, which almost everyone has experienced to some degree over the years. We need to understand what to do with this time or how to reap the benefits of it, or we risk falling into an unproductive brain spiral and giving up.

In addition, I didn't connect with the practice of reflection for a long time because it was foreign to my faith tradition. Reflective practices are more common in contemplative traditions of faith. Growing up evangelical and charismatic, I have found that our practices are often communal, active, and noisy. We like loud music, loud services, and loud people. These were my spiritual comfort foods, and they continue to nourish me. But I was rarely given time to sit, reflect, and think. As a result, I didn't see the point.

These are just a few reasons why the practice of reflection can send most of us running for the hills.

> I didn't connect with the practice of reflection for a long time because it was foreign to my faith tradition. Reflective practices are more common in contemplative traditions of faith. Growing up evangelical and charismatic, I have found that our practices are often communal, active, and noisy.

The Power of Personal Reflection

Those who practice reflection unlock multiple superpowers God has for us.

1. Reflection helps us regain control over the state of our minds.

We are probably suffering from the most attention deficit period in our lives. It isn't just a genetic trait affecting a sliver of the population. According to a survey by Microsoft, the average human attention span in the year 2000 was twelve seconds. Today, it has shrunk to eight seconds.[3] As our capacity for attention wanes, it is increasingly difficult for us to focus our minds. Our brains are being whipped from one thing to the next, often feeling outside our control.

Personal Reflection is a powerful way to bridle our minds. It allows us to take conscious control over directing our thoughts and what we meditate on. It shakes us out of our frantic mode and puts intentionality back into our thinking. The more we practice this, the better we become at directing our thoughts where we want them to go.

2. Reflection allows us to learn in a fast-paced life.

As I mentioned earlier, we can easily find ourselves repeating the same mistakes over and over again. Personal Reflection gives us what we need to learn from our mistakes. While it doesn't solve all our problems, it does help us understand them. It teaches us what patterns we've been following. It can help us understand where they originated. Perhaps we've been looking for solutions in the wrong places—it can show us that. When we feel a bit crazy for getting stuck in a destructive cycle again, reflection can shine a flashlight on what's happening, revealing the true problem, and pointing us toward a solution.

3. Reflection can help us resolve negative emotions.

As Personal Reflection helps us understand our experiences, it can also be a gateway to healing for all negative experiences and emotions. For example, while an unkind word may stick with us throughout the day, reflection may allow us to see that the other person was dealing with a terrible problem. This doesn't excuse their behavior, but it can help us manage our emotional reactions so we don't let someone else's words control us. This is one example, but there are countless others.

Sometimes just being able to put words to what has happened and how we felt is enough to release our brains from the spiral of fear, bitterness, or being overwhelmed. This practice keeps us from dwelling on negative experiences for long and allows us to heal more quickly from offenses. Ultimately, it produces emotional strength and buoyancy in us. This is the core of spiritual resiliency.

4. Reflection helps us position ourselves for the future.

I believe God created us to live meaningful lives, but it is a challenge to live a faithful life daily. We are simply not paying attention to many areas of our lives. Without reflecting, I have poor peripheral vision and see only what's in front of me. But when we engage in regular reflection, we can consider the things not in our immediate purview.

Faithfulness does not happen by accident. It takes deliberate consideration of the most important things. Personal Reflection helps us push back against the flow that chaos brings into our lives. Reflection is the rudder of a ship before it hits full speed, pointing our lives in the right direction.

How to Practice Personal Reflection

Step 1: Schedule checkpoints for reflection.

Looking at my calendar, you may see blocks of time titled "Think about Family" or "Think about Marriage." I have scheduled times to think and reflect on critical areas of my life. In addition, my wife and I have built a habit of reflecting together at the end of our days and weeks. These slated times help me make sure life is not moving faster than I can manage.

This may mean carving out time in the morning, evening, on your weekly Micro-Retreat, on date night, or in your community. When can you set a regular habit of reflection in your day and/or week?

Step 2: Start with a brain dump.

In the Micro-Retreat chapter, I introduced a tool I learned from my therapist called "Morning Pages." To reiterate, it's a brain dump to write out our stream of consciousness. By doing this, we skim off all the loudest and most preeminent brain chatter so our minds can move on to other thoughts. Once we skim off the surface thoughts, we can move past that layer of our minds and hearts to expose what is hidden inside. While this step is a bit of a precursor, we can already learn a great deal by observing what we've dumped onto the page.

Step 3: Recount events.

Ask yourself, "What did I do?" "What happened?" Often, I list the significant events from the last week, or even just the last twenty-four hours, depending on how long I have. If an event held particular significance, I write it out in more detail, noting who was there, what happened, and how I felt.

The Power of Journaling

If you're like me, your mind on any given day is scattered. One minute I'm thinking about what to do at work and the next, I'm wondering where I left my keys. It makes it effortful to reflect when we try to do it all in our minds. We'll lose our train of thought the second a dog walks by. Our thoughts become so nebulous that by the end of our time, we can feel unsure of what we accomplished and whether any of it made sense. For this reason, our minds benefit from having handles to hold onto as we reflect; we need to translate our intangible, internal thoughts into a tangible, external form.

One powerful way to do this is to write our reflections down in a journal. The process of writing organizes our thoughts. Instead of our brain firing off in random directions, we have to write in sentences. That natural writing process—even if we don't feel we're good at it—can bring an extraordinary amount of clarity to our thoughts.

Journaling can be done with paper and pen (highly recommended) or a digital journal. It just needs to be a medium where you can put thoughts from your brain onto something else. A bulk of research shows that our brains process and cement what we handwrite far better than if we type it. However you choose to do it, journaling is a powerful habit to hold and protect our reflections.

Step 4: Seek God's perspective.

Reflection is not just a personal experience; it is a *prayerful* experience. That makes reflection a spiritual practice instead of a mental exercise that anyone of any faith (or no faith) might do. It is done with the Spirit of God in mind. When I am open to God, I discover a different perspective on circumstances that gives me more insight into my choices.

After I recount in my day, I will often ask God, "What do you think of this? Why did this happen? Why did I feel this way? Is there something you saw that I didn't see?" At that point, I will sit still and allow God to breathe new insights into my mind. As fresh thoughts come, I write them down, knowing I can test and discern the words later.

Reflect with Others

There are some things we cannot process thoroughly alone. Sometimes, we need the care of another person to anchor us in reality, especially when dealing with painful experiences or memories that send our brains into panic mode. Other times, we need someone to point out our blind spots or encourage us in what we've already learned. And for the verbal processors out there, sometimes the act of forming thoughts into words before another person is enough to spark fresh realization.

Beyond this, reflecting in community allows us to see larger patterns when other people's experiences are similar to ours. Sometimes this is beneficial to do before journaling, and sometimes it's helpful to do after, depending on how your brain processes best.

However you do it, processing with your spiritual community is a powerful way to reflect in the presence of those who also carry God's Spirit. If you have the right people around you, they can help bring your reflections into more powerful places.

Personal Reflection is an indispensable tool for developing clarity and emotional resilience. This powerful tool in the practice will help us think more clearly, handle the craziness of life around us, and point our lives toward God.

Listening Prayer: Amidst a Thousand Voices, Only One Matters

*While theology should inform a Christian's relationship
with God, it should never take its place.*
HENRY T. BLACKABY,
HEARING GOD'S VOICE

*Prayer is not monologue, but dialogue; God's voice is
its most essential part. Listening to God's voice is the
secret of the assurance that He will listen to mine.*
ANDY MURRAY

I felt called to ministry at an early age. Following this path, I eventually needed to decide where to go to seminary. It was a big decision and a monumental moment in my life.

So much pressure was riding on this decision. It would inform where I would spend an extensive amount of my time. I had to scrounge up the money to pay for it. Additionally, most schools I wanted to attend were out of state. I had never lived outside of Chicago, where I grew up. This was going to be a life-altering shift.

I did my due diligence. I researched each school, considered their tuition costs, and stalked their Twitter accounts. I explored the graduates' lives from those schools to see if their culture resonated with me. I researched their doctrines of faith. I investigated their programs to see if they matched what I felt God was doing in my life. I compiled pages and pages of research and notes, and still, I didn't know what to do! I thought the information would help me make an "informed" choice. That's what information is for, right? Still, I had no idea what to do. Application deadlines loomed.

Weary of processing this decision, the unique qualities of each school started blurring together, like mixing a bunch of colors until they looked like mud. I was experiencing decision fatigue and the pressure of needing to decide, juxtaposed with the fear of making the wrong choice.

In exasperation, I threw my research pages on the floor, got on my knees, and cried out to God, "I don't know where to go! I've done my part and still don't have answers. You know where I should go. Can you tell me where to go?"

I was on my knees praying to God with wrinkled papers scattered around me. And I heard something unexpected. It was not a sound but a feeling that arose within me—a feeling I remembered so clearly from crucial moments throughout my Christian walk. It was the same feeling I felt when I gave my life to Jesus many years before. That feeling accompanied me through my highest and lowest of times. Like a warm winter coat, the feeling began enveloping me and surrounding me. It was the feeling of God's presence.

In that presence, an impression came to my spirit as clear as day. And it simply said, "Go to Fuller Seminary." I didn't understand this impression because, on paper, it made the least sense. Fuller was the farthest away—1,741 miles, to be exact, from Chicago to Los Angeles.

It was the place where I knew absolutely no one. On top of everything else, it was the most expensive. In short, it was the one that required the most of me. Yet the impression felt so clear. It was the voice of peace, love, and guidance. In my heart that day, on my knees before God, I decided. "Lord, if you want me to go there, I will."

The next ten-plus years would find me in Southern California at one of the top seminaries in the world. If you have ever been in a situation like this before, you'll understand when I say this: God's blessing was far above and beyond what I could have ever imagined. I grew tremendously. I met my wife in Los Angeles, found a great church, and I am currently raising my kids here. I'm still reaping the benefits of this decision.

It happened to be one of the best decisions I've ever made in my life. The irony of it all? I didn't choose it. I believe that God chose it. I just walked into it.

When life feels hectic, do you ever have trouble figuring out where to go next?

When there's great complexity in our internal and external world, it's difficult to make decisions. We hear many voices: the voices of our social circles, public opinion, and those inside our heads. How do we manage all the things we hear? It is common to feel lost. The story I just shared was my first exposure to the power of Listening Prayer for a key decision in the midst of overwhelm.

Have you "heard God speak" before? I place quotations around this because hearing is more of a metaphor to describe a sense of divine communication that doesn't fit well into our language or intellectual paradigms. While some experience God's leading through an audible voice, we typically say hearing to describe the widespread phenomenon of sensing, intuiting, or experiencing God's leading.

Hearing God's voice carries a variety of interpretations. Some believe God speaks through the Word, but they have trouble believing we can really claim to know God's perspective for our everyday situations. Others see hearing God's voice as monumental, once-or-twice-in-a-lifetime encounters, usually reserved for missionaries and church conferences. Each of these is valid. However, I don't believe hearing from God must be limited to either of these interpretations. In addition to the Word, I believe God loves to guide us in real-time, as we see throughout scripture. I also believe God loves to communicate with us in a whisper to our hearts in the mundane days. The Lord often gifts us with clarity, revelation, encouragement, or direction when we are bold enough to ask—especially when we reach out in need.

> Listening Prayer is the practice of tuning in to God's still, small voice so we know what to do in a storm.

I often experience God's voice as a thought planted in my brain at just the right moment—one that doesn't originate from my human logic. Sometimes it's a feeling of peace, a realization, a fresh conviction, remembering a Bible verse, a timely encouragement from another, an image that forms in my mind, or even just a gentle reminder that I am loved and God is with me. I then try to fit these impressions into human words as I scribble in my journal.

There is biblical precedent for this type of regular, intimate communication. One example is in John 10:14, when Jesus says, "I am the good shepherd. I know my own and my own know me." When Jesus describes his relationship with us, he uses the analogy of sheep. He is the shepherd, and we are the sheep. And we are to hear the voice of the shepherd.

Because of that verse, there are wonderful pictures of the shepherd and wooly sheep in antique and Christian stores. Maybe it evokes a sense of fuzzy warmth and kindness. However, the description of us being sheep conveys something about us—sheep are not the brightest creatures. They are not intelligent. A sheep doesn't understand the geography of its region, it doesn't correlate cause and effect, and it doesn't think critically about its place in life.

Beyond that, they have no defense mechanisms. They are completely helpless. They follow the other sheep around them. Several years ago, there was a news report that five hundred Turkish sheep had fallen off a cliff and died.[4] Can you imagine the horror of seeing that many sheep drop like flies? Do you know how it started? It began with one sheep that went astray—all the others followed suit.

Some people read the famous passage in John 10 and feel slightly offended. We're much more intelligent than this herd animal. The comparison insults our autonomy, flying in the face of what the world tells us about ourselves. It says that we are competent, advanced, and self-sufficient. We don't simply follow the person in front of us. Or do we?

The flaw in this line of thought is the assumption that we can figure everything out ourselves. The truth is this, despite how great we are, we are still extremely limited. There are things in the cosmos that we have absolutely no idea about, just as a single sheep in Texas could not fathom Antarctica. For all our advancement as a species, we must never forget that we have barely scratched the surface of God's created order.

However, sheep have a redemptive quality: they are adept at hearing the voice of their shepherd. Like in the passage, a flock of sheep stands idle at the sound of a stranger's call. Their ability to follow the shepherd's voice leads them where they're supposed to go despite their minuscule perspective. To embrace my identity as a simple sheep is so freeing. It reminds me that for all our modern advancements, my shortcomings, and the chaos around me, I only need to be good at hearing the voice of my shepherd.

My experience of picking which seminary to attend continues to inform and encourage me. I don't know all the answers, and that's okay. But if I focus on leaning into God and hearing his heart, I know I'll be okay. That is never a call for negligence or for not taking decisions seriously. But at the end of the day, hearing the shepherd's voice is enough to get us through the complexities of life.

The Power of Listening Prayer

Let me share why it's so freeing to rely on our shepherd's voice as we develop resilience.

1. Listening Prayer frees us from the pressure to know everything.

The pressure to know absolutely and to make informed decisions is sometimes nerve-racking. We gather data, ask around for opinions, and overanalyze everything. Regardless, we'll never know every possible angle or comprehend every data point.

That's why the image of sheep is most comforting. Sheep have no concept of their pen. They have no comprehension of the hunting behavior of wolves. They can't grasp the seasons of growth for the grass. All they know is their shepherd's voice. And somehow, that's enough. It's always enough.

Psalm 119 gives an illustration to describe the nature of hearing from God. "Your word is a lamp to my feet and a light to my path." It imagines following God akin to someone holding a lamp in the darkness trying to find their way and where to go. The light illuminates, but just enough to see where their feet are going. God never meant for us to see that far—just far enough to take the next step. God leads us little by little.

2. Listening Prayer shifts our attention to the most valuable perspective.

Gathering opinions is so great. I always use Yelp when trying out a new restaurant. I want to know what people think of an establishment before I go. But sometimes, hearing people's opinions is exhausting. The need to appease people occasionally drives us to seek out every voice on every subject. And worse still, those voices conflict! And everyone has strong opinions. What do we do?

Ultimately, I need God's voice to cut through people's opinions. My shepherd knows my situation, who I am, and his calling on my life. That opinion matters to me most; it pierces through the noise to give me direction.

3. Listening Prayer helps us release control over outcomes.

There is so much pressure to get our decisions right. Under this pressure, we forget there is a God in the universe who continues to make it hang. We forget that our shepherd is gracious and holds us even when we have no idea what we're doing.

Hearing God's voice allows us to make decisions and leave the results up to God. It frees us from the anxiety of needing everything to fall into the right place. At the end of the day, if God tells us to do something, we trust that God will see the results through, even if it's different from how we imagined them.

> Hearing God's voice allows us to make decisions and leave the results up to God. It frees us from the anxiety of needing everything to fall into the right place.

How to Practice Listening Prayer

A note before you go on:

People often ask, "How do I know it's God's voice?" For me, it's similar to the experience of a new friend calling for the first time. When you answer and they say, "Hello," you have to ask who it is. (At least in the age before Caller ID). But if they keep calling you, you begin to recognize them by the sound of their voice. Over time, you can pick their unique sound out of a crowd. You become familiar with their verbiage, mannerisms, and accent. In the same way, we become more attuned to the tone, vocabulary, and substance of God's voice as we practice listening.

So how do we practice listening? I will share just one way, based on my experience and study of the scriptures. These four steps have reliably guided me and many others by creating a space where we can be receptive.

Remember: God wants to speak to us. Hearing is not for the perfect, the spiritually elite, or given as a reward for good behavior. In this exercise, take a step of faith to believe God wants to unlock new understanding, clarity, and comfort to meet you right where you are.

Step 1: Seek an environment suitable for hearing.

We must remember that for most people, the voice of God is not thunder but a *whisper*. The story that inspires me is about Elijah in 1 Kings 19. Elijah hears a whisper. *That was how God chose to speak to him.* If you want to hear God more regularly, find spaces to pray where a whisper can be heard.

My spaces include a Prayer Walk, sitting in my car, waking up before my children, visiting a garden, a coffee shop, or a retreat. It also means I resist filling already quiet spaces with a noise like turning on the television every evening, playing music or a podcast while driving, or scrolling on my lunch break. Consider what quiet spots you can cultivate to hear his whisper.

Step 2: Ask God specific questions.

God hears the heart that's pressing in and ready to receive. Often, I will ask God to speak very specifically into an area of my life. The more specific the questions, the more precise the answers. Ask questions about specific areas of life or concerns of your heart:

"God, what do you think about my job?"

"God, what do you think about me right now?"

"God, what do you think about my leadership at work?"
"God, what do you want me to focus on today?"
"God, how should I respond to this person?"

Step 3: Be attentive to words, phrases, or images that may come to mind.

God speaks in multiple ways when we engage in this manner. Listen for words and phrases that come to your spirit. Be open for Bible verses to pop into your head. Pay attention to pictures or images. You may be surprised by what comes to mind during your time with God. Don't dismiss it. Just write it down.

I ask for clarification when I receive a word or image I don't immediately understand. "What do you mean by this, God?" This prolongs the conversation, and God will often speak more about it. Sometimes I won't receive confirmation until later, through another word from God, words spoken by another person, or an event that takes place. If I'm still unsure, I do my best and trust he will course-correct me if I get something wrong. Over time, it becomes easier to identify what rings true to God's character and scripture compared to what falls flat.

Step 4: Discern against scripture, God's character, and community.

While hearing from God personally is beautiful, you must check what you've heard with God-given accountability sources to make sure you heard right. There have been many times I've thought I heard God's voice, but in the end, it was my perspective and desires I was projecting onto God. Or I did hear something accurately but lacked the maturity to apply it well. Or I lacked the biblical knowledge to fit that insight into the larger thread of my Christian ethics.

I have found it wise to hold what I've heard in my spirit against three main God-given sources of truth checking.

The first is the Bible. Nothing I've heard in my time with God should contradict what is in God's word. As a Christian, the more mature your faith becomes, and the more you read the scriptures, the easier you can judge whether what you hear is congruent with the Bible God gave you.

The second is the knowledge of God's character. The most apparent contradiction to God's character is when hearing voices of condemnation or shame. We may struggle with differentiating these voices especially if an authority figure in our faith has shamed us. However, this is inconsistent with God's character. He corrects and disciplines his children but does not shame or condemn us. We can practice correcting ourselves with scriptures and truths about his character.

The third is to check with our communities. Contrary to our Western ideals of individualism, God did not intend that we enact our faith alone. Our communities can confirm what we're hearing, correct us, or give us a different perspective to see through. It's best for us to share with our small groups, spiritual mentors, or pastors.

Listening Prayer is a declaration that amid a thousand voices, only one truly matters. This practice helps us remain connected and navigate the world as God's sheep staying close to our shepherd.

Confronting Our Inner World

*The only one who possesses interior peace can
efficaciously help his neighbor. How can I communicate
this peace to others, if I myself do not have it?*
PHILIPPE, REV. JACQUES

*A sure way of retaining the grace of heaven is to disregard
outward appearances, and diligently to cultivate such things
as foster amendment of life and fervour of soul, rather
than to cultivate those qualities that seem most popular.*
THOMAS À KEMPIS, THE INNER LIFE

The first two years of my marriage were extremely difficult. I didn't
know how to manage my stress, and it didn't take much for me
to become irritated. That irritation often found its outlet in the place I
felt the safest—in my home and with my wife.

We tend to have a go-to emotional response to stress. There are
various ways we respond without self-control or self-awareness.
Typical responses are running away, storming out of the room, or

emotionally disengaging and distancing from others. Giving the silent treatment is a good example of this response. Other common reactions are to zone out, disappear into social media, daydream, or pretend nothing is wrong.

My knee-jerk response was to blame myself and become defensive or focus the blame on others. Yet I didn't realize my blaming attitude was the byproduct of something deeper and more effortful to pinpoint. Consciously, I simply believed my life would improve when my wife got it right. I wouldn't lash out verbally if she would just stop doing the things that upset me.

For obvious reasons, we ended up in marriage counseling. Here's my memory of that first session.

Esther and I settled into the gray, padded chairs across from the counselor sitting behind her desk. When it was my turn, I presented my case.

I remember how the counselor listened to me patiently, nodding in response to my emphatic perspective that I was in the right and that Esther needed to change. Judging by her face, I was sure she saw my perspective and would help Esther come around. But when she spoke, she said, "Phil, I understand you're upset, and I'm curious about what you're planning to do when you're upset?"

I was taken aback. I thought this conversation was going to be about my wife! I felt justified in my critical outbursts. I stammered, "Why are we focusing on me and not her?"

She said quite bluntly, "Well, because you can't control her. You can control yourself."

That didn't go as planned!

From that session forward, the most valuable thing I learned was how important it was to own my emotional state. Emotional and spiritual maturity is recognizing that while I couldn't control what my wife did or didn't do, I could control my response. I was utterly responsible for managing the state of my own heart and how I chose to treat her. It was much easier to blame than take ownership of the emotional atmosphere I cultivated in my home.

The same is true of our relationship with the world in which we live. We can blame our world and circumstances, living a narrative that says someone or something can steal our peace. We can bemoan our helplessness and wish we could escape it, but the truth is that we cannot change or control anything or anyone. We can only control how we respond, how we tend our hearts, how we treat others, what attitude we bring, and what environment we cultivate.

In order to take ownership of our inner well-being, we need to develop a rhythm of confronting what's inside of us. Confronting is a call to pay attention to our inner life. To face this means that once we have left (gotten alone) and are still, we must dig deeper into the state of our hearts. We must examine the deeper things there—wounds, dreams, memories, etc. Those seeds tucked deeply inside us wield influence over our actions, whether or not we realize it. We must confront these things if we are to take ownership of our emotional and spiritual state.

> In order to take ownership of our inner well-being, we need to develop a rhythm of confronting what's inside of us.

While this is undoubtedly challenging, it's exactly what Jesus modeled for us as he consistently went to God in prayer with the innermost depths of his heart. We live in a world without peace that needs peacemakers. It's a world of anger that needs love. But how can we bring peace to others when we're not at peace with ourselves? How can we love those who frighten or anger us when we are unaware of the fear and anger buried inside? How can we share hope when in our deepest place, we are in despair? We must know ourselves more accurately, more authentically. This is where we get to be the salt and light of the world.

The ultimate goal of this rhythm is not self-awareness for its own sake. As we face ourselves in our most authentic states, we give God the opportunity to bring change and healing into our lives. As the spiritual practices in this section demonstrate, we progress from confronting ourselves to boldly expressing our pain which ushers us into a place to encounter God. The transformation we experience redefines who we are and how we behave. When we return to our regular contexts, we will be more equipped to impact the world for God's purposes.

How Confronting Creates Resilience

1. Confronting gives us a space to offer up our wounds to God.

Jesus is a healer. He heals our lives' pains, wounds, anger, and brokenness. But that healing doesn't come to us without our participation. Jesus doesn't promise to wave a magic wand in the air and have all our internal brokenness disappear. Instead, in partnership with the Holy Spirit, our eyes are open to our life's deep and hidden things. Divine healing occurs when we offer our hurting places to God in honesty and vulnerability. Confronting is about holding our brokenness up to the healer of souls. Only then can we partner with the one who can make all things right within us.

2. Confronting allows us to express our deepest emotions of lament, regret, and grief.

It's common for us to feel uncomfortable with displays of despair or grief. We may want to jump ahead too quickly from experiencing the genuine losses that come with life. We may also confuse lament with intercessory prayer, petitioning God to take action. But lament is not action oriented. Rather, it simply expresses loss, regret, and despair.

The Bible is filled with examples of lament and anguished cries to God that expressed feelings but did not expect a different outcome. We understand that situations have occurred that cannot be changed or will not be altered. We cannot undo a death, a grievance, or an injustice. Here, we cry out to God and receive comfort knowing that Jesus, familiar with suffering, grieves alongside us.

3. Confronting allows God to transform us through a spiritual encounter.

The purpose of the spiritual practices in this book is to make space for us to encounter God and allow him to transform us into the likeness of Christ. Without the actual transformation of the Holy Spirit, these practices are helpful psychologically, but not spiritually. We cannot force God to meet with us, but we can position ourselves to be more aware and open to what God wants to do in our lives.

Four Practices for Confronting

The following practices revolve around exposing our hearts before God to be transformed. Each of these practices is engineered for immeasurable resilience, bolstering us to live in the world as healed people. Here are four practices for confronting you will find in the following chapters.

Practice 7: Heart Check
Practice 8: Holy Lament
Practice 9: Identity Meditation
Practice 10: Encounter Worship

Heart Check:
Managing Messy Emotions

*We must do our business faithfully; without trouble or
disquiet, recalling our mind to God mildly, and with
tranquility, as often as we find it wandering from Him.*
BROTHER LAWRENCE

*Silence promotes the presence of God, prevents many harsh
and proud words, and suppresses many dangers in the way
of ridiculing or harshly judging our neighbors…If you are
faithful on keeping silence when it is not necessary to speak,
God will preserve you from evil when it is right for you to talk.*
FRANCOIS FENELON, 17TH CENTURY

With eyes furrowed, I ate my food silently amongst my family. My wife, sensing something amiss, asked, "Are you okay?"

"Yes," I said abruptly, fully aware of the untruth. We continued to eat in silence. The children caught the drift that something was off, and they adapted, eating lunch quietly together.

As we were cleaning up after lunch, my wife chastised me. "You sucked the life out of the room during lunch today."

I paused, thought, and nodded, "Yes, you're right. I'm sorry."

I knew something was off in me—I felt grouchy and distant. Yet I wasn't quite sure what it was. It was as if I was experiencing a symptom, but I couldn't identify the cause.

I went upstairs and spent time in quiet. As I sat and asked God to help me understand my foul mood, a memory floated to the surface of my mind. It seemed so foolish at the time, but I couldn't stop thinking of an event that happened at work earlier. During a meeting, I was continually interrupted from speaking by different people. The meeting concluded hastily with no opportunity for me to share my thoughts.

I sat, pen and paper in hand, with a scribbled prompt. "What are you feeling?" Eyes closed, nodding slowly, I began to understand. I wrote down beneath the question, "unheard and overlooked."

Ah, I'd found the root of the symptom now. It had nothing to do with my family at lunch. There was something deeper at play, something that had lodged itself into my heart and influenced my actions. I hadn't even been aware of it before, but I was grateful I stopped to confront it and now understood what it was.

Often in the Bible, various writers compare our hearts to a garden. Gardens can be beautiful, and they can be unruly. They have a variety of living organisms growing inside them, balanced in a careful ecosystem. People can plant things, and they can uproot them. If they tend the garden well, it can be beautiful and vibrant. If they don't, the plot can grow wild, and weeds can choke out the good, fruitful plants.

If our heart is like a garden, everything we experience plants a seed in it. Sometimes, we have great experiences that plant beautiful flowers and fruit trees. Other times, we have painful, frustrating, or disappointing experiences that plant seeds of hurt. These are comparable to a weed or invasive species that live alongside good plants. If we continue to let the bad seeds go unchecked, they will continue to grow. Over time, they produce bad fruit in our lives—like impatience, irritation, anger, judgment, etc. They can even threaten to overtake good plants if we don't keep them in check, as they will always keep growing if we don't prune them.

This practice, the Heart-Check, is a way of tending the garden of our hearts. In the story I shared above, an experience from my day had planted a bad seed in me. Because I hadn't paid attention to it, it had grown throughout the day and produced grouchiness and withdrawal in me. When I confronted that feeling, I could identify what was growing there and what experience had planted it. Having identified the source, I could take the feelings of being unseen and unheard by God, process them with my wife, reorient my perspective, and choose my next steps.

> Heart-Check is a practice to tend to our emotions, identify their sources, and submit them to God for healing.

When you are in a heated moment, this is a practice to guide your hearts, minds, and souls into a peaceful place before you live in ways you will regret. Ultimately, this process develops invaluable emotional maturity in us, allowing our inner lives to be healthy and thriving, capable of handling anything.

The Power of The Heart Check

1. The Heart Check keeps our emotions from being the masters of our lives.

Emotions are great guides but terrible masters.

We as Christians recognize that our emotions are a gift. God gave us our hearts to feel and to experience life with. But we also understand that our emotions are not everything. They are certainly not God. In the heat of the moment, they often obscure our perspective, which is already limited to begin with. We spiral and struggle because we can't see the truth, yet we have access to the one who gives us the right perspective.

Therefore, it is important to assess and analyze, "What does God say about this feeling and this action?" Just as 2 Corinthians 10:5 says, "We take captive every thought to make it obedient to Christ." Paul's exhortation in this verse is not to be ruled by what lies within us. Instead, we are to take captive the things we feel and turn them over to the lordship of Jesus.

2. The Heart-Check addresses the core of our emotions.

Our world has many strategies for circumventing negative emotions. During the pandemic, one industry that skyrocketed was entertainment companies. Whether it was Disney or Netflix, entertainment company shares went through the roof.[5] Most people numb themselves in response to a world of pain, confusion, and chaos.

However, at the core of these emotions is a God-given need that hasn't been satisfied in a godly way. The Heart-Check is powerful because it addresses it at the core level, not the surface. It is not a band-aid—it's a tool to invite us to look at the deepest parts of our hearts.

3. The Heart Check relies on the Maker of our hearts for its healing and wholeness.

Emotions are a gift from God. More importantly, God designed them. And if God created them, then he has the user manual. We cannot fully study mental and emotional health without the leadership of the One who made both.

God also made us and understands us perfectly. Psalm 139 says that God knit us in our mother's womb. That means God has carefully crafted every single fiber, cell, and emotion. He knows our ins and outs. Even if other people don't understand us, even if people think we're crazy, God knows us. And if that is true, my heart and emotional healing starts with God. It begins with talking and dialoguing intimately with the One who made us.

The Heart-Check is powerful in that it incorporates a dialogue with God. It invites God into partnership with us to bring our hearts to a whole and healthy place.

> Even if other people don't understand us, even if people think we're crazy, God knows us. And if that is true, my heart and emotional healing starts with God.

How to Practice the Heart Check

Step 1: Take yourself out of the heat.

This is the principle as outlined in the chapter on leaving. We have to leave the heat to see what's taken root in us to produce the emotions we're feeling.

Can you find a place away from all the noise and rancor for a few moments? Can you find a comfy chair in a quiet place where you can reflect? Sometimes it helps me to sit on a couch, turn off the lights, and just sit in darkness and silence. That allows me to stop paying attention to all the external stimuli distracting me and to create an environment to focus inward.

Step 2: Ask yourself, "What am I feeling?"

The principle at play is this: name your emotions, tame your emotions. Whatever you can't name, you can't control. But once you can name it, your brain has an "ah-ha" moment, and you can now understand it.

When you understand it, you can walk forward armed with the right response.

The more specifically you can label an emotion, the more power you will have over it. Feeling bad versus feeling depressed, feeling disappointed versus feeling rejected—the latter examples are more helpful because they are more specific and give you a better idea of how to respond. Try searching "The Feelings Wheel" online to find a helpful tool for putting language to emotions.

Step 3: Ask yourself, "Why am I feeling this?"

Understanding an emotion's origin point provides us even more power and future insight as to what events trigger them.

"This person said _____ to me, and now I feel hurt."

"The project went way over budget, and now I am stressed."

"Being on social media and seeing what people are doing makes me feel depressed about my life."

For this to be effective, we need to focus more on describing what happened rather than assigning blame to others or ourselves.

Step 4: Ask yourself, "What have I done (or can I do) when I feel this way?"

We tend to develop habits in response to certain emotions, but those habits aren't always helpful to us. What actions are you tempted to do because you feel these emotions? What actions have you taken in the past because you felt these emotions? What do other people do when they feel these emotions? Understanding that will be critical in cutting off unhelpful patterns that may exist. Thinking this through will give you ideas of how to respond differently.

Step 5: Ask yourself, "What does God say about this?"

Take time in prayer to listen to the Holy Spirit and ask what to do. Listen for a new perspective on the situation, something you may have missed, a truth to soothe your fears, a truth about the other person. Meditate on scriptures relevant to your emotion. Turn every emotion over to God's lordship.

Step 6: Ask yourself, "What do I need at this moment?"

At the center of our healing is recognizing a core need. A core need is a God-given desire at the center of our hearts. Consider what it is that you desire at the core. If you feel hurt, then your core need may be respect or love. If you feel stressed, then perhaps your core need is peace. What is your core need?

Step 7: Ask the Holy Spirit, "Holy Spirit, can you help me?"

Pray the prayer, "Holy Spirit, can you help me? Can you help me to live like Jesus in this moment?" We need to pray earnestly for God's help so we can have his strength and grace. It is a prayerful submission that garners the strength and grace of God.

As we face numerous experiences daily, they plant both good and bad seeds in our hearts. Whether we like it or even realize it, if these are left untended, they will grow and manifest in our actions. When we practice the Heart Check, we confront our emotions, understand the root of them, and submit them to God for the healing of our souls.

Holy Lament:
Sharing Our Suffering in Safety

*I am not a theologian or a scholar, but I am very aware of the
fact that pain is necessary to all of us. In my own life, I think
I can honestly say that out of the deepest pain has come the
strongest conviction of the presence of God and the love of God.*

ELISABETH ELLIOT

I f someone read certain pages of my journals, they would think I'm
not a Christian.

I have filled much of my journals with gratitude, processing, and
planning for the future. But some pages are not written in the bright,
optimistic, "let go and let God" attitude our Christian culture has
come to expect of one another. Penned on days when my heart had
been wrung dry, many pages of my journal are filled with swearing,
despairing, and questioning. These are my pages of lament, and they
are as holy as any other.

In our current culture, this practice is more pertinent than ever. Access to the world's despair, suffering, and injustice is as easy as the tap of a button on our phones. Images too horrible to digest can drop us to our knees in disgust and agony. The more we become aware of our own failings and how we have harmed others, especially those we love the most, the more anguish builds. Most often, we continue to scroll because we simply have no idea how to process it.

What do we do with our pain? There is no shortage of coping mechanisms that we as a society have developed. Whether it's eating, binging television, social media, or substances, we all have our outlets for pain. But many of us find that the world's ways of handling pain often don't help us. They lead us down paths to where we, in some shape or form, become more corrupt than when we first started.

Our American culture does not teach us to lament well. In America, we have the funeral service, but no formal way of facilitating the grieving process beyond that point. In biblical times, people marked their grief by wearing sackcloth and ashes, and there were professional mourners—people who grieved alongside the grieving as an actual job—and played instruments or sang chants to indicate a period of mourning. What do we have in our context? Too often, we have simplistic, chipper answers. Many who are too uncomfortable to endure suffering treat it like a hot potato they must quickly toss away.

When we turn to the church, we discover the overwhelming majority of our worship songs are happy, grateful, triumphant, and declarative. Often, I have wanted to sing them, but they felt like a lie in my throat. I trusted God—I wanted to be near to him. I wasn't turning my back on him, but I had rage and sorrow in me. For so long, I felt like I needed to choose. I could mourn, rage, and grieve, or be in his presence. It wasn't until I learned about the practice of lament that I discovered the truth: I did not need to choose.

I learned a great deal from Jesus's example of lament in the following verses:

Jesus took Peter and the two sons of Zebedee with Him and began to be grieved and distressed. Then He said to them, "My soul is deeply grieved, to the point of death; remain here and keep watch with Me." And He went a little beyond them, and fell on His face and prayed, saying, "My Father, if it is possible, let this cup pass from Me…" Matthew 26:36–46

At this point, Jesus was enduring an excruciating time in his life. He knew that very soon he would go to the cross. Of the many things Jesus did in his life, I find this scene to be one of the most moving. We see a different side of Jesus, a more vulnerable, even desperate Jesus. When he cried, "Abba," his cry was not one of a savior, a teacher, or a healer. It was the cry of a son before his father. It was full of sorrow, pain, and confusion. It was an expression of utter soul-wrenching grief. A moment of sweating blood and weeping tears. Somehow, none of this was antithetical to the fact that this was Jesus, the Son of God. The Son of God, in the garden, pleading for there to be another way. This raw expression of lament preceded the clarity Jesus received when he willingly went to the cross.

In Jesus's most critical and painful hour, lament was his practice of choice. In that example, even in his dying moments, we learn that lament is our God-given way to express the deepest grief of our heart—without ever separating us from God, even for a second.

> Holy Lament is a form of prayer where we bring our grief, pain, and rage to God as a form of intimacy and worship.

Holy Lament is very different from other types of prayer, like intercession, which focuses on an outcome. Lament has no outcome in mind. It is not vying for God to do something in response. It's a cry of anguish over what has happened and what most often cannot be undone. Lament is our God-given space to pray, "I don't feel you right now. I don't know what you're doing in my life. Where have you gone?" It is an expression from the depths of our heart, the primary pain outlet for the Christian.

All this time, I didn't realize that the Bible and the traditions that followed it provided an outlet for dealing with all the pain we experience regularly. Did you know about seventy percent of the Psalms are not praises but laments? They contain complaints, cries, and even curses. While the modern evangelical church tends to let it gather dust in the corner, discovering the practice of Holy Lament was a new form of freedom for me.

The Power of Holy Lament

There are a few key reasons that Holy Lament wields this transformative power.

1. Lament provides us with a space to express our deepest pain.

The heart needs to be fully known to be free.

I love kids because you never have to guess what they're thinking. If they are upset, you can tell. You can watch their body language. The wincing in their eyes. The stamping of their feet. The pouting of their lips. The slinking of their shoulders. Yet, at some point, they stop showing their true selves. At some point, kids become old enough to do what adults have learned to do—to put on a mask.

Holy Lament is an invitation to be brutally honest again. We can see this in Jesus's cry. He asked his Father in that moment, "Why have you forsaken me?" Twice! To the ears of a Christian, it strikes us that Jesus would question the presence of his omnipresent Father. Yet anyone who has wrestled with the human condition would know exactly what Jesus was doing—he was crying out from the depths of his human experience.

The heart cry is like a child pounding on their father's chest asking, "Why?" It is not an act of rebellion; it is an act of faith in the resilience of our Father's bosom. He can take the gut-wrenching cries of his children. God can handle your honesty.

2. Lament brings pain to its rightful place.

Holy Lament is the practice of bringing our pain to God, the one who can handle it.

We often try to place our pain upon things or people who do not have the power to heal it. We may over-rely on our friends, partners, entertainment, or social media, trying to find someone to carry our pain with us. However, even the best of friends or partners cannot be the ones who heal us.

Another option is keeping our pain inside, where it only evolves further. When left unaddressed, pain becomes something altogether different. Pain becomes anger, discontentment, jadedness, and hopelessness. Undealt with emotional pain is like poison to our soul. In real life, there is a "broken heart syndrome." Mayo Clinic's definition: "People with broken heart syndrome may have sudden chest pain or think they're having a heart attack." The heart in emotional pain has actual physical manifestations. A heart held closed is a heart that is dying. Like a child, we can never truly deny the heart's pains. That type of pain never goes away; it finds different outlets to express itself.

But as Jesus cried out to the Father, he showed us where pain belongs. It belongs to the ears of our Heavenly Father. It doesn't belong on social media or with our spouses or peers. It belongs in the ears and heart of the One who fashioned it, who knows us intimately and desires to connect with us at the deepest levels.

> When left unaddressed, pain becomes something altogether different. Pain becomes anger, discontentment, jadedness, and hopelessness. Undealt with emotional pain is like poison to our soul.

3. Lament positions us to be embraced by love.

Our gut-wrenching prayers are not given as words into the air, just to fall to the ground. Rather, they reach the ears of the One expecting our eager and childlike cry.

How does God respond to lament? By embracing back. I cannot help but think of the father in the story of the prodigal son in Luke 15. The son totally abandoned his father. But in the son's misery and brokenness, he finally turns around and decides to return home. Yet as the son comes home, contrite and bitter toward himself, the father is waiting for him.

It says the father ran. In those days, the father would be wearing a robe. The image of a Jewish father, as noble as he was, hiking up his skirt, and running through the fields to his son's embrace, was scandalous. It was an embarrassment. Yet with tears probably running down the father's face, we see now what lay in his heart. The father's heart was revealed as wide open, willing to endure embarrassment because love held a higher demand. The heart finds its wholeness in the arms of a father who loves us unconditionally.

How to Practice Holy Lament

Step 1: Find a private place.

To properly lament, I need to be in a space where I can be completely alone and free. That may mean locking your door or getting in your car if your home has little privacy.

Step 2: Pray prayers that have no words.

Lament is less intellectual and more physical. When you lament, I encourage you to explore the spectrum of emotional expression that

God has given you. Shout, scream, yell, or weep. These are all welcomed expressions of lament in the Psalms.

There are many times I will be on my knees before God groaning. It is because, as Romans 8:26 says, the Spirit inside of us is "groaning too deep for words." Maybe I will say a word or two—a simple "Lord." Or just say his name, "Jesus." Whatever is in your heart, let that be your prayer. Let it be raw, honest, and authentic to the Father.

Lament Through Journaling

Sometimes, when we approach lament, we feel dry and numb, unsure of how to start. Especially if we feel this way, it can be too hard to sit still. One of the things I do is journal my pain. I talk to God about it, write openly and honestly, and use the most accurate, raw, and transparent language that I can. You can do the same. Name your feelings. The act of writing itself prompts your brain to process the words in a new way. Seeing them on a page validates that they are real and helps you clarify what you feel and why.

Step 3: Pray a Psalm of lament.

If you have no words, then use the ones already written. I have found reading a Psalm has given me words I didn't have myself. Here are some you can pray:

- Psalm 3
- Psalm 6
- Psalm 13
- Psalm 22
- Psalm 25
- Psalm 31

- Psalm 44
- Psalm 86
- Psalm 142

Step 4: Spend time listening.

Sometimes the cry is enough itself. But other times, I hear whispers of God's voice. These are such raw and intimate moments, to realize in a tangible way that God is present in our pain. Try to spend a few moments after lamenting to listen to what our Father may say.

In a world of pain, people will turn to all sorts of release valves, but none of these ways genuinely help. Holy Lament is a practice that allows our hearts to express themselves to the ears of God and in complete and open honesty. Whenever you feel pain, and you will, practice lament.

Identity Meditation: Remembering Who Determines Our Worth

The greatest trap in our life is not success, popularity or power, but self-rejection.

HENRI NOUWEN

We must understand that God does not "love" us without liking us—through gritted teeth—as "Christian" love is sometimes thought to do. Rather, out of the eternal freshness of his perpetually self-renewed being, the heavenly Father cherishes the earth and each human being upon it.

DALLAS WILLARD

The other day, I opened my social media. In my suggested friends list, I saw the face of one of the kids from the youth ministry I led years ago. I tapped their profile, and I'm sure the surprise was evident on my face. Next to the smiling face of this young kid was a very, very large number. This kid had hundreds and thousands of followers. "They have so much influence; they could start selling products!" I thought to myself as I scoured their page, noting the many likes and comments.

I feel embarrassed to admit this, but as I scrolled through this kid's social media account, I felt like a total loser. *Why don't people follow me? Am I not interesting or important?* I suddenly didn't feel confident or sure of myself.

Do you ever come across situations that make you feel like a nobody? I come across them constantly. I encounter this in the clothes I wear, what jobs I pursue, and what friends I keep around me. It gets triggered when I see someone do something cool or have an awesome job while I'm stuck at my "lame" one. In some shape or form, at every turn, my soul asks, "Who am I? Am I important? Am I significant?" Chaos exposes our insecurities. In an already fragile state, the world says everyone's doing something significant but me.

By both nature and nurture, I am an achiever. I am a go-getter who prides myself on my efficiency and productivity. I work and work as a way of soothing my insecurities. I assuage my self-doubt with the accomplishments I've won. And like most people find out the hard way, no achievement can fill the gaping hole.

The way Jesus roots himself in his identity is radically different. I discovered this by observing the Father's delight in Jesus's life in Matthew 3:16:

> And when Jesus was baptized, immediately he went up from the water, and behold, the heavens were opened to him, and he saw the Spirit of God descending like a dove and coming to rest on him, and behold, a voice from heaven said, "This is my beloved Son, with whom I am well pleased."

Then, as John the Baptist baptized Jesus, the heavens opened. And Father God bellows below his opinion of this Jesus who has done nothing. What does God say? What does the Father of Creation say to Jesus with nothing on his resume? He says this:

"This is my beloved Son, with whom I am well pleased."

What powerful words. As they resounded from heaven, all those in witness heard these precious words. Who is Jesus? In this spectacle, Jesus demonstrates to us how identity is given; God gives it!

The most remarkable thing about God's delight in Jesus is his timing. Jesus has not taught anyone, healed a single person, or raised a human from the dead, and he has not discipled anyone. Jesus, at this point, has done absolutely nothing. Jesus was not a prophet, a healer, a teacher, or a discipler—he was just the child of God. And still, the Father pours out his pleasure over him simply because Jesus is his Son.

That became the strength of Jesus' life. It became the solid rock beneath his ministry. He didn't work for a place of worth; he worked *from* a place of worth. He refused when people wanted to make him king (John 3). He cast away the devil and his temptations of power and fame. Jesus was not crushed by his success nor impoverished by his apparent lack thereof. That identity was forged in a place of nothingness.

> Identity Meditation is the practice of securing our sense of self through God's affection rather than through our own work.

To become anchored in my God-given identity, I practice sitting in spaces where I have nothing to work on, nothing to accomplish. I feel naked. There's no one else to praise or reassure me. With these things absent, all that's left is me. Just me. For the length of my solitude, I begin to see the trophies I've dreamed of and earned mean nothing. They are nothing to him. Compared to his greatness, there is no trophy I could shine that would compare to his glory.

And so, I am just as I am, having nothing before God. As I sit there in silence, counting my breaths, growing my awareness of

God's presence in and around me, a deconstruction happens. It is the deconstruction of my identity being wrapped up in the things I do.

This deconstruction is something I resisted before. It works against all my comforts and natural instincts. Yet now, as I learn to sit in his presence and learn the truth that my soul needs to hear repeated, I still feel naked—he can see everything in me. But God's voice removes the fear and shame from that feeling of nakedness. Without shame, being naked is just being seen. He sees me, and he accepts me as I am. I am loved; therefore, I am successful. Not the other way around.

The Power of Identity Meditation

1. Identity Meditation disconnects our accomplishments from God's approval.

Behind so many people's busy calendars, endless activities, a plethora of relationships, and myriad pursuits is a person who does not know who they are. Busyness is often a veil for the lack of value we feel. So when we lose a job, relationship, an opportunity, or perceive that we have failed at something, our sense of identity can spiral. These changes are even more common in chaotic times when the world is so in flux. We can look to other people to tell us who we are, which is a precarious way to build a sense of self.

> Busyness is often a veil for the lack of value we feel. So when we lose a job, relationship, an opportunity, or perceive that we have failed at something, our sense of identity can spiral.

Identity Meditation allows us to construct a sense of self that does not crumble when our role or circumstance changes. It helps us divorce our sense of worth from our productivity.

2. Identity Meditation anchors us in the One who defines our identity.

So many people walk around in life with a deep question, "Who am I? Am I valuable? Am I my job? Am I a parent? Am I a worker? Who am I?" These questions plague us, even till we are older. And we end up chasing after the things we hope will define who we are. Throughout generations, society has attempted (and failed) to answer that question.

We fail to understand who we are because we ask the wrong question. The answer to that question is simple. Who we are is simply a product of *whose* we are. Our identity is in relationship to our Heavenly Father. Just like the things we make, the identity of an object is in the design and intention of the Maker. In the same way, to sit before our Heavenly Father is to sit in the presence of the one who can speak into our identity.

Identity Meditation is powerful because it is time we spend in the presence of the One who made us. It is in God's presence that our identity cup gets filled. It is in that space, with all our insecurities, where we long and wait to hear what our Maker would say of us. In that space, our hearts search for value and identity is met by the only one who can complete it.

3. Identity Meditation allows our souls to be truly enjoyed.

Deep inside our soul is a desire for someone of importance and value to see us for who we are and to say to us, "You are important and enjoyed." I feel that Jesus sensed this need. And as he was baptized, he heard those beautiful words that all of us long to hear. He was one in whom God was "well pleased." At the heart of the one searching for identity is one who longs for those words.

One of the things I do in Identity Meditation is to sit there in nothingness and ask God, "What do you see when you see me? What do you feel when you look at me? What do you think of me, Father?"

Many times I will hear, "You are my son." Those meditations have led me to hear some of the most precious words that my soul has ever heard. I feel that I am completely invincible after hearing what God says of me. No task, job, or no harsh word from another could sway me about my sense of self-worth. It is not because I have spoken it myself. It is because God has spoken it over me. And his enjoyment of my life fills the cup of my identity.

How to Practice Identity Meditation

Step 1: Go somewhere your securities cannot be found.

The beginning of Identity Meditation starts with removing ourselves from that which typically makes up our identity. What are the places that you are tempted to draw identity from? Family? Work? School? Friends? "Withdraw" from those things by being in spaces where those things are absent. Go away from anything that we might use as a proxy for our security. We must be naked before God, absent of the things used to impress others. Much like the other practices, I go somewhere quiet and in nature.

Step 2: Acknowledge insecurity.

In the secret places of our hearts, we all tell stories of how unimpressive we are. What are the stories that you unconsciously tell? Mine are:

"I'm not impressive."

"I'm a nobody."

"I'm not significant."

"I'm not doing anything important."

"I don't have what it takes."

What are the things that make you feel unimportant and unvalued? What is it that makes you feel insecure? Hold these thoughts for a moment. We spend so much time pushing them down or trying to soothe them with accomplishments, praise, wealth, and influence. Just let them rise to the surface so you can look at them for a moment.

Step 3: Receive God's delight over you.

Whatever thoughts you were holding from step two, recognize that God loves you most in this precise state. It is hard for us to understand this because we are surrounded by a world that seeks validation in what we can add to our lives. There is nothing that you can add to your life that can make him love you less or more.

Take the insecurities listed in step 2, then fill them into this prayer. You can pray it aloud or write it in your journal.

"Thank you that, despite _____, you love me."

"Thank you, even though I haven't done _____, you delight in me."

"Thank you that even though _____, you enjoy and like me."

"Thank you that amid _____, you are proud of me."

Step 4: Ask God to show you how he sees you.

Ask God some deliberate questions.

"Lord, what do you think of me?"

"What did you like about me when you made me?"

"What do you enjoy about me that others don't?"

I encourage you to write down what comes to your mind in this space. These are not self-aggrandizing or conceited questions to ask. These are the questions of a child asking their parent to define them rather than letting the world have that job. God longs to answer.

Take time to listen and be cognizant of God's presence. Enjoy and participate in divine friendship.

∽

In a world of counterfeit identities, people will chase after the things that make them feel secure. Ironically, this only makes our sense of self more unstable. The way we counteract this is to position ourselves before the God who determines our true worth. By sitting and hearing his words of identity over our lives, we walk in the footsteps of Jesus who did the same. These words protect our hearts from frivolous activity and give us certainty in who we are as we reenter a chaotic world.

PRACTICE 10

Encounter Worship:
Opening to Transformation

I need to worship because without it I can forget that I have a
big God beside me and live in fear. I need to worship because
without it I can forget his calling and begin to live in a spirit
of self-preoccupation. I need to worship because without it
I lose a sense of wonder and gratitude and plod through life
with blinders on. I need worship because my natural tendency
is toward self-reliance and stubborn independence.

JOHN ORTBERG

We should know and celebrate God with our whole
person. While too many Christians neglect to serve
God with the mind, others cultivate only their minds
and neglect the emotional aspects of worship.

CRAIG S. KEENER

I was in the study of my house. In this period of life—single and a student—I was going through a very tumultuous time. Between school, work responsibilities, and church ministry, it seemed like everything was caving in around me. My stress levels were extremely high, and I was at the point of breaking.

In this stress, I suddenly felt the nudge I believe was from God: *Lay down and worship me.*

I wasn't sure what to do, but I obeyed. I put my headphones on, blasted worship music, lay on the floor on my back, and just worshiped God.

I squeezed my eyes tight and tried to imagine his face in my mind; I tried to imagine his piercing yet gentle eyes and the light coming from his face. Whispering to myself, I declared truths about who he was.

The strangest thing happened. Like an ice cube under the summer sun, the stress began to melt away. I was overcome by something larger. My stressors felt so overwhelming mere minutes ago, but now, compared to the greatness of God's glory, they seemed puny.

A sense of joy began welling up within me, and I started laughing. I couldn't help it; the laughter came out naturally. I felt God's joy and love ooze over my entire body. I could feel my pressures come back into perspective—they no longer threatened to overtake me because I had a refreshed sense that God was with me in the storm.

This act of worship allowed me to behold the presence of God above the presence of my pressures. It led me to fixate on his face, and it shifted my whole internal world to orbit his truth again.

As a worship leader at church for much of my life, I thought I knew a lot about worship. I could lead groups of people through the flow of a worship set. I understood that worship was a time to shift our eyes from ourselves to God. I knew it was not about us, and our worship was a gift we give God because he is worthy. But before this, I didn't understand the power of worship intersecting with the chaos of our daily life. It wasn't until this one day that the power of worship for chaos became personal.

I was used to leaving my chaos at home and entering the spiritual bubble of church before worshipping. However, I realized that I only knew how to worship from the shore for so much of my life. So when I was in the middle of my storm, I subconsciously thought I needed to get to the safety of the shore to worship. That moment was life-changing because God directed me to worship while I was in the eye of the storm. I did not need to wait to catch up with God when the week slowed down. Singing out in his presence while lying in the middle of all my papers, pressures, to-dos, and fears revealed God's power not just to change my circumstances but to change who I was within them.

That was where the power of worship came in. From that day forth, I realized that worship was not just a song. It was a tool to protect me against the crushing pressures around me and forge resilience in my soul to handle them. I now regularly practice this form of worship, which I call "Encounter Worship," to combat overly challenging situations in and around my life.

What exactly is Encounter Worship?

> Encounter Worship is a form of worship that focuses on beholding God's glory for victory over chaotic situations around us.

There is a story in the Bible that forms the inspiration for Encounter Worship and how it can help us turn the tide. We see its power in the book of Acts when Paul and Silas were in prison for preaching the gospel. They were living in horrible conditions. It was dark, dirty, and full of pests and disease. The omen of death loomed. They were chained, awaiting their death. Yet Acts 16:25 describes how they sang hymns in prison as the other prisoners listened to their praises. They prayed and sang to God with joy. Despite their circumstances, they decided to fix their eyes on who God is and declared his character.

What happens next? Acts 16:26 says, "Suddenly there was a great earthquake so that the foundations of the prison were shaken. And immediately all the doors were opened, and everyone's bonds were unfastened." The jailers were deathly afraid and wanted to know this God who freed their prisoners. Talk about a turnaround situation!

What set this into motion was Paul and Silas choosing to worship God. Despite them being in a terrible situation, the resilience in their spirit allowed them to worship in a way that changed the atmosphere in and around them.

The Power of Encounter Worship

What does worship do when we are in chaos? It has three powers in its weaponry.

1. The songs we sing are instructional for our soul.

The songs we sing in worship are declarations, pleas, and adorations. But something we don't often recognize is that they are also instructional. By that, I mean we don't just sing the words because we feel them. In a way, particularly in chaos, we sing the words as if we are teaching our souls that they are true. As we sing, our hearts are formed and shaped into the reality of our words. As the sounds reverberate in our lungs, those truths shape our souls.

This understanding was common among the Israelites. They didn't just contain songs of adoration but also the stories and lessons of God. Families taught their children what God was like and what he had done for their people through songs sung in their homes. In singing, we instruct our souls, teaching and reminding ourselves of critical truths about God's character.

2. Worship realigns us with God's rhythms.

In earlier rhythms like Personal Reflection, Lament, and Heart Check, we focused on understanding ourselves and our hearts with God's guidance. But in this practice, we turn our attention away from ourselves and toward our God. We move from confronting what's in our hearts to confronting who God is.

We enter God's presence, and we're often surprised by how powerfully he encounters us. In Encounter Worship, we remember that God is here to be experienced; we only need to turn and look to him. In the power of his presence, we fall into his rhythms rather than trying to forge our own. Even before our circumstances change, we are internally transformed and strengthened.

3. Worship brings a physical and spiritual shift in our environment.

Recently, my wife and I were having a rough day. It was in the heat of summer with scorching temperatures of one hundred degrees or more. Amid already stressful work and family situations, our air conditioner broke! It was sweltering in the house, and my wife was pregnant. Our attitudes could have been better.

We had just picked up our girls from school, and they were happily at play in the playroom. My wife and I were trying to stay cool and not be so miserable. Suddenly, one of my girls, while playing Legos, started singing songs she learned from school:

Our God is an awesome God,
He reigns from heaven above,
With wisdom, power, and love,
Our God is an awesome God.

Our other daughter joined in. Then the toddler began babbling away, pretending to sing. They kept singing that song over and over again. My wife and I took notice, and suddenly, the atmosphere of the room started shifting. All of us slowly joined in. Instead of being miserable and grumpy, we started bursting with joy. Even though it was still hot, the room was filled with laughter, joy, and adoration of God.

Every place has a spiritual atmosphere. Every place is a unique spiritual environment whether it's your workplace, school, or neighborhood. Frequently in chaos, that environment is filled with worry, stress, and anxiety. Worship has the power to change that atmosphere.

Fill Contentious Places with Worship

In 2 Chronicles 20, we see that when king Jehosephat was about to engage in a fierce battle, he put his singers, musicians, and worshipers in the front of the battle. He wanted his people to calibrate and worship God even before the battle began. Following this spirit, God invites us to enter contentious places with worship at the forefront. I believe that if we worship in spaces where there is chaos, it changes the spiritual atmosphere of that space.

If family life is chaotic, fill every room with the sound of praise. If your work is crazy, get in at work before everyone else and worship in that space. There is something powerful about worship in spaces parched of God's presence.

How to Practice Encounter Worship

Encountering God in worship is not about chasing after a fleeting emotional high. Instead, it is about coming into a space where our hearts, minds, and souls come into alignment with the greatness of God. And when they come in alignment, we find that hopelessness, despair, and anxiety wash away like a flood.

Step 1: Play worship music.

Find a song online, put on some headphones, and just listen. Have the same song play over and over again. Many people criticize how modern worship songs are very repetitive. If worship was purely about reciting theology, then repetition would be problematic. However, I believe there is a specific method to this repetition, seeing how the heavenly beings say the same thing repeatedly (Revelation 4). Repetition is a form of meditation that engrains the truth into our brains until we begin to believe it and live by it more readily.

God may invite you to worship with lyrics of your own. Sometimes there are seasons when a song is resonating in our hearts for a reason. Usually, it's because God is inviting us to interact with him in a certain way and he wants to reveal himself to us.

Step 2: Bring your body into worship.

Worship throughout the Bible is a very physically involved activity. We are called to lift hands (Psalm 134:2), to dance (Psalm 149:3), to lay flat (Psalm 95:6), to sing (Psalm 47:6), to shout (Psalm 27:6), and on and on. For all the variance in postures of worship, they are meant to usher our spirits into a different dimension. They point to the truth that outward action changes our internal hearts.

Following this truth, find ways to worship with your body. Maybe that means opening your hands, putting a hand on your heart, dancing, laying down, lifting your arms, kneeling, etc. I believe many would experience God in a new way if they were not too embarrassed or self-conscious to dance.

Step 3: Start with thanksgiving.

Psalm 100 says to "Enter his gates with thanksgiving." Start with praise, thanksgiving, and gratitude. Think of your day, week, and life, and list your prayers of thanksgiving. Praise God amid whatever emotions you may be feeling. List God's character traits and speak adoration. "Thank you that you are holy. Thank you that you are wonderful. Lord, we say that you are powerful!"

We are fast becoming a culture obsessing over our feelings, issues, and needs. God cares about each of these dearly. But in worship, we can shift our focus from ourselves to God. And the powerful thing is that when we put hosting God's presence first and focus on him, he takes care of us.

Step 4: Position yourself to receive.

Ultimately, we cannot control the outcome of our times in worship. We cannot control what God chooses to do inside us or in our situations. However, we can certainly position ourselves to receive whatever God wants to do at this time.

To do this, pray, "God, come have your way in me and the world around me." Invite God to encounter your spirit and bring you back into his rhythm.

Until The Breakthrough Comes

Rees Howell, one of the most famous intercessors, often said he would "worship until the victory was won inside of his heart." In charismatic circles, we call that "breakthrough." Often the phenomenon of breakthrough refers to a shift felt in our emotions or spirit. For example, if we're praying for fear, anxiety, or worry to leave, we experience the breakthrough when we sense those things leaving us. Instead, we then feel a fresh sense of how mighty God is, and we feel joy, hope, and power come to replace fear. This internal breakthrough often leads to external breakthroughs, leading us to act differently.

That said, we do not need an emotional experience to validate our worship or its power in ourselves and our surroundings. Sometimes we experience the fruit of our choice to worship in the moment, or we may experience its fruits later on. Ultimately, we cannot control how the tangible outcome of our worship looks, and that does not invalidate it in any way. Whatever it looks like, the fact remains that worship is a powerful expression that strengthens our spirit with resilience for the things ahead.

Worship is the re-centering of our minds, hearts, and souls on the greatness of God. The practice reminds us of God's truths, realigns us to God's rhythms, and influences the atmosphere around us.

Returning to the World

So far, the spiritual practices I've described in this book have focused on removing ourselves from others and having the opportunity to experience God's presence and healing power. Whether it's taking a Micro-Retreat, taking a walk, being still, or meditating on our identity, it involves us being away from our context, at least for a moment. These are proven to be lifesavers.

God can do much in a person's life when we open ourselves to transformation through spiritual practices. We have the story of Moses, who spent time with God on the mountaintop. When he returned to the valley below, his face shone with such brightness that no one could safely look at him. Moses had to cover his face.

> God can do much in a person's life when we open ourselves to transformation through spiritual practices.

While it's unlikely that our faces will shine to such an extent, it is quite common for us to return from an encounter with God with a glow that we'd not had before. We may have insight into ourselves that alter the way we treat others or change our decisions for our future.

I suspect Moses would have preferred to stay on the mountain with God than come back to deal with the grumbling Israelites in the valley.

But we can't stay there forever, and we can't run from every problem. At some point, we must reenter the world. We return to our families, friends, work, and the places where chaos still rages. In these moments, it can feel like all our growth has evaporated into thin air. I've come back from a Micro-Retreat fully refreshed and invigorated, but the next day, fall back into a pattern of being far from God. How did this happen?

It is one thing to receive something from God; it is a whole other thing to hold it.

There's another challenge as well. The first time I returned from a retreat, I had a very difficult time putting my experience into words. It wasn't that my wife and friends weren't interested in what had occurred for me. It was that I had experienced such a profound connection with God that I had trouble translating something so personal to someone else. This rhythm focuses on how to return to "ordinary" life after having an extraordinary experience—something we want to share with others.

Yet this step—perhaps the most challenging—is exactly what we are called to as Christians. We were never meant to stay in the bubble. Once we have been transformed, it's our call to reenter our contexts as transformed people. When we are changed, we naturally change the spheres around us.

How do we persist? How do we keep the fire burning? How do we nurture what we've received? That is where the practices of returning come in.

How Returning Well Creates Resilience

1. Returning teaches us that our faith must be integrative.

The mountaintop experiences do not measure the authenticity of our faith. Our faith is tested in the day-to-day minutiae of life. I believe God will speak to you powerfully in Micro-Retreats, moments of reflection, and silence. But we are also meant to be changed people when we're at our kids' soccer practice, when there's a contentious meeting at work, or when the world is screaming about a news event. In these moments, rather than becoming part of the chaos, we become a force of resilience and wholeness. Ultimately, this challenges us to believe that God is alive and powerful in every sphere of our lives.

2. Returning well teaches us to steward what God has spoken.

In our times alone with him, God plants seeds of patience, hope, kindness, healing, understanding, etc. in us. Afterward, we choose whether we nurture it or let it die off. What good is it if God spoke to you about your marriage, and you come home and forget what he spoke? If God starts growing patience in me on my retreat, but I keep letting my road rage go unchecked, the seed of patience will die. If he speaks identity over me, but I believe what someone else says instead, the transformation he started in me will be stunted. When God gifts us revelation, insight, and wisdom, he expects that we are fruitful and faithful to it.

Being fruitful and faithful means applying it to our lives and producing the effect that God intended to produce. The practice of returning helps us to steward and grow the things that God graciously gave us.

3. Returning well allows us to be the salt and light we are meant to be in the world.

The gifts God gives us were never meant to stay within us. Like a tree that bears fruit, the fruit is meant to feed the hungry. When we experience healing, we live in the world as healed people. When we have rhythms of resilience, our thriving naturally overflows to the Church and our non-Christian world. That allows others around us to experience healing too. After all, Christianity is not a basin, it's a river. The work of God should overflow from our lives onto the lives of others.

There have been times when I've come back from a Personal Retreat, returned to work, and talked to my non-Christian workers about the things that God spoke to me. They don't fully understand everything I'm saying, but they notice my patience when everyone else is complaining. They notice my kindness when they make a mistake. They notice my humility when I apologize for my own mistakes. It's God's presence in me. Returning well is about the spirituality that allows us to be perpetual light and salt in our chaotic world.

Five Practices for Returning

Here are five practices to keep the fire burning in the midst of chaos.

Practice 11: Fellowship
Practice 12: Sabbath Dinner
Practice 13: Story Listening
Practice 14: The Enemy Blessing
Practice 15: One-Second Prayers

Fellowship:
Finding Friends for the Fire

*Show me your five closest friends; I'll
show you your next five years.*

UNKNOWN

*Behold, how good and pleasant it is when brothers
dwell in unity! It is like the precious oil on the head.*

PSALM 133

*Satan always hates Christian fellowship; it is his
policy to keep Christians apart. Anything which can
divide saints from one another he delights in.*

CHARLES SPURGEON

One of my most memorable times of Fellowship was in March 2020 when the pandemic hit. Right when everything was about to go south, I felt led to call my friend Eric to hang out. We walked together down a wide pathway at 5:30 in the morning—the only time we could manage with our jobs, spouses, and multiple kids.

We spent over an hour talking, praying, and challenging each other. He talked about the fear of needing to shut his business down. I talked about my concerns about taking care of my family. As the sun was coming up that morning, we listened to each other, discerned God's will for each other, prayed, and gave each other words of encouragement and direction we were sensing from the Lord.

This walk turned out to be one of the most influential for the next couple of years. Like storing away food for a long winter, the food of connection that morning sustained me through the chaos of the pandemic. We remarked on how timely and accurate the words we heard from God were for each other. We heard words and prayers for one another that resonated so deeply and powerfully that it lasted us multiple seasons.

It was a relationship that sustained me and challenged me. It was, among a few others, a relationship that pushed me toward righteousness, godliness, and my purpose in God. To this day we are friends, pushing each other toward the great things God has for us.

One of the most common sentiments people tell me in chaos is how lonely they feel.

Whether it's dealing with the craziness of parenting, jobs, or dealing with national crises, people feel isolated and alone. We become so busy trying to put out fires in our lives, we often neglect to reach out to others. We begin to develop a belief that others wouldn't understand or that we'd be a burden. Our thoughts, struggles, and isolation are hard on our souls. We have no one to process with, making matters worse. Over time, we dwindle in our loneliness.

How ironic that we are the most connected generation, yet people can still feel so alone? We can tap friends from almost anywhere on planet earth at any time of the day. People are available via text messaging, email, and social media, yet they feel further than ever. We feel deeply misunderstood, under-supported, and hopelessly alone.

Worse, I find that the older I become the fewer friends I have. This certainly isn't the case for everyone—it may have something to do with my full-time job, four children, and book writing. Regardless, it is not uncommon for people to live more solitary lives as they get older.

Though I value community, I sometimes feel the pull to do my own thing, especially when the world is on fire. I make unfair generalizations about people. I can lean into the tribalization that's taking place—a magnetization of people toward those who agree with them. Particularly in these times, it's easy to make "enemies" of people, or entire groups of people we have never even had a conversation with.

Even when we do connect with others, it's tempting to remain at a surface level. We can mistake talking and hanging out together for genuine Fellowship. Yet God is calling his people to be different. To thrive in tumultuous times, I believe God is telling the church to *lean into community*. There is something that sets Fellowship apart from the casual relationships we may already have in plenty.

What exactly is Fellowship?

Fellowship is the practice of gathering with other believers under Christ's presence to fuel one another toward faithful living.

Fellowship is powerful. In a world divided and separated, the words of Hebrews 10:25 echo to us today, "Do not give up meeting together, as some are in the habit of doing, but encouraging one another—and all the more as you see the Day approaching." The epistles' readers are spread about the lands due to the persecution starting in the Roman Empire. And while they have moved and relocated and are in new homes, he still encourages them to keep meeting. They are still to break bread, meet for Bible study, gather for worship, and organize serving together. In chaos and even persecution, they are to draw closer together, not further away.

Paul also urges them to continue meeting as "they see the Day approaching." While there's a lot more that could be said about this, the gist is that "the Day" is in reference to the return of Jesus. It is a period they are anticipating will be even more chaotic. And as this day approaches, their Fellowship is all the *more* meaningful.

Anyone not in Fellowship is especially vulnerable to the forces of chaos. There is no one to encourage them or comfort them, to hear their questions or doubts, or to lament alongside them. There is no one to see their lives, offer accountability, show them a different perspective, or dream with them. Like an animal that has left the herd, they are left alone to the world's dangers. They become a target of our enemy, striking them as they wander alone. It is the holy community that allows them to be shielded, guarded, and fruitful in the crazy world we live in.

The Power of Fellowship

Unfortunately, not every friend helps us in the fire. We have all experienced relationships that have drained us, discouraged us, and even brought us into a worse place. Perhaps you feel tempted to be alone because the Fellowship you've experienced has been a poor one.

What are the relationships that help us in the fire of chaos? What are the friendships that the Bible envisages when it speaks of the Fellowship that helps us prepare even for the day of Jesus's coming? In my experience, there are three types of relationships that keep us centered through chaos.

1. Fellowship gives us people in our corner.

Everyone needs friends who are in their corner. Friends in our corner are not simply people we have fun and hang out with, though that's an important element of friendship. Friends in our corner engage with us on a deeper level, see who we are meant to be, and actively champion our growth. In doing so, they create safe spaces for us to be raw, messy, and vulnerable. They believe in us even when we fail. We need people who can stand with us in our darkest moments and represent the presence of Christ to us.

2. Fellowship gives us friends who call us higher.

One evening, my friends observed a conversation between me and my wife. We were conversing about how I act a certain way when I'm stressed, and she was challenging me to improve. My friend, who didn't know this was normal in my relationship with my wife, said jokingly, "Oooooh, she's calling you out, Phil!"

I laughed with him, but said, "No, we don't do that in our marriage. We don't call each other out; we call each other *up*."

Our culture is becoming fascinated with calling each other out. It is a tactic of shaming publicly, condemning people for their wrong actions. It usually happens outside the context of a real relationship. But that doesn't help them become the people God intended them to be.

I believe what we need as Christians is for people to call us *up*. We need friends who call us to a higher standard. We need people to look us in the eye and say, "You can do better. God made you for greater things than this." We need people who can see what God wants to do in us and help us realize it even when we're not there yet. This is a component of Fellowship.

3. Fellowship gives us friends who make our blood boil.

I know, this sounds crazy, but hear me out. Whenever there is public chaos, the endless news cycle becomes increasingly adept and fascinated with creating enemies on which to blame our problems. They focus on narratives about how bad other people are, and how they are the enemy.

I'll be the first to admit that having people around me who are on the "other side" is not easy. It's challenging when they are people we go to church or Bible study with or are our neighbors. *How can you think this way? Why would you value that? Are you crazy to believe that?* These questions constantly come to mind, and I can become standoffish.

But do you know what I've learned? God keeps these people in my life for a reason—for my growth.

It is so tempting to make our Christian community one of people who simply like us and tell us what we already believe. In chaos, people want to surround themselves with others who think exactly like them so they don't have to deal with others' differences.

However, this is not the community that God intended. We are not a tribe that draws boundary lines based on how the world does it. We need to remind ourselves that Jesus called both Judas Iscariot, an employee of the Roman Empire, and Simon the Zealot, one who was zealous for overthrowing the Roman Empire, into the same discipleship group! Can you picture the kind of side conversations they had? Can you imagine how appealing it must have been to find out who each were and where they stood?

Yet in their journey following Christ, I believe God divinely used their friction to shape them to be more like him. Despite our natural inclinations, we need friends that make our blood boil. The things we boil about often indicate ways we need to grow and allow God to chisel us into his likeness.

Joining the Body

Hebrews commands us not to give up meeting together. I have found that almost everyone I talk to who is struggling spiritually to survive in chaos has one thing in common—they are not plugged into a local church. The enemy of our soul preys on people, like sheep, who are wandering, trying to figure out life independently.

It sounds simple, but there is power in committing to a local church. It is the power of being in a community where we are on the same page and the work of God is calling us toward himself. Sit under the preaching of the word. As hard as it is these days, do the discipline of committing to community. Give to and receive from your community, and you will find that God gives grace for you to thrive through the fire of your life.

I know, especially in recent years, so many have been wounded from others in the Church. If that's you, I am so sorry. I have experienced this and understand your hesitation to dive in again. Still, don't go at it alone. I pray you find a community of people who can love you well and support you as you process.

How to Practice Fellowship

Step 1: Make a list of three to five people in your life who push you higher.

Jesus had concentric circles of friendships in his life. He had the three (Peter, James, and John). He had the twelve (disciples). He had the seventy-two he sent out (Luke 10:1–23). Then there were the crowds that followed him. The smaller the circle, the closer he was to them. He invited only Peter, James, and John into the most intimate moments of his life, such as his transfiguration and his time in the garden before the cross.

If Jesus had three buddies, we could use three buddies. I truly believe in every season, God places a few individuals in our lives to call us higher.

Maybe you're already clear on who your inner circle is, or perhaps you don't have a close one in this season of life (I've been there). Regardless, take a minute and consider who in your life wants to grow with and shape you. Write down their names.

Step 2: Meet with them and go deep.

Intimacy provides depth. If you're sick of small talk, like I am, take your small group of friends into more intimate settings for deep conversation. As a married man, I fill this group with other men. I regularly and proactively ask these people to go on walks with me, grab a late-night snack, or even get groceries.

Part of the joy of Fellowship comes from the ability to laugh, hang out, and feel comfortable together. However, the point of Fellowship isn't *only* to hang out at a surface level, even if it's fun. The point is to go beyond that—to go deep. Just as we joke around, we ask each other hard questions that no one else in our lives will ask. Here are common questions that fuel us:

"What are you struggling with?"

"How is your relationship with God?"

"How is your character?"

"How can I pray for you?"

"How is your marriage? How are you serving your wife?"

"What is God doing in your life this season?"

The deeper the conversation, the more fuel I have to face the chaos of my life.

Step 3: Speak words of encouragement whenever you can.

Don't just a be receiver of encouragement, be a builder.

On Sundays at church service, I make it a point to try to encourage people around me. It can be as simple as, "Bless you brother," or "God loves you."

So many people in the thick of the chaos of their lives aren't looking for advice. They're just looking for someone who can look them in the eyes and say, "Keep going." "You can do it." Be that person for your church. Create a space where everyone has friends in their corner.

Step 4: Fight for the longevity of the relationship.

Some friendships are to shape us for a season of our lives, but others are to last throughout multiple seasons or even a lifetime. Yet we must anticipate that conflict is inevitable. If undealt with, it can create distance. Also, when someone sees us at our worst, it can feel very vulnerable; we may be tempted to pull away or allow natural distance to draw us apart.

I know it's hard, but if God gives you grace, commit to remaining connected to certain people. Even when you experience conflict or one of you moves or has a baby, and there's no time anymore, a quick text now and then can be just what they need. Ask God who these people are in your life and write their names down.

Spiritual Mentors

In the chaos of my life, I often don't see the larger picture. I am currently in a season of parenting young kids. It can feel crazy sometimes. For this reason, I make it a point to find spiritual mentors, particularly people a few life stages ahead of me.

Find people who have walked in your shoes. I meet with men with grown kids who can give me perspective on parenting young ones. Often, they offer me perspectives or strategies I wouldn't have figured out for years. No one will have your exact scenario, but some people likely have a decent familiarity with the road you're walking. Look in your local church. In my experience, people are looking to invest in someone.

Note: Don't go into these relationships with a "serve me" approach. Go into them, even those you're expecting mentorship from, with a "how can I serve you?" attitude. Take them out to lunch. Pray for them. I make a point to treat them as people who need friendship too. I ask them how their life is going. I buy gifts for them. That lets them know that this is a genuine friendship, not just a one-way relationship.

Friendships in the modern age are complicated. Even though we are exposed and more connected than ever, we become lonelier and lonelier. We must avoid the temptations of our enemy to operate life alone. In times of chaos, we need the rich moments of Fellowship that God designed. Strong, powerful godly relationships fuel our faith.

PRACTICE 12

Sabbath Dinner: The Celebration to Resist an Anxious World

*When we cease from pursuing our material goals for one day
each week, we're saying, 'God, I trust You to ... provide for my
needs seven days a week even if I only work for six of them.'*
ROBERT SHAW

I was sitting with my life group on a Friday night. We were gathered
around a long rectangular table—one that reminded me of those
depicted in paintings of the disciples sitting together (a table my wife
and I specifically purchased for this reason). The smell of grilled
chicken, roasted veggies, and other savory fragrances filled the room.
Everyone was getting seated, awaiting the time when we would start
eating together.

As everyone got situated, people shared and reflected on their
hectic weeks. Someone apologized for being late because of the
doomsday L.A. traffic. Another shared how they were running behind
on looming projects and it was causing them stress. One person talked

about the crisis they had at work and how they had to spend overtime helping an employee experiencing domestic violence get placed in a safe house. My wife and I shared our challenges of parenting and home life that week.

At the end of the table, I started the festivities. I gathered everyone's attention and set the tone for our dinner. "Sabbath Dinner is first a celebration. Despite all our crazy weeks, the fact that we're here, breathing and eating is evidence that God has freed us from all the pressures this week has placed on us."

The room let out a collective sigh. Despite their busy weeks, we were doing what we sometimes cannot do in the frenzy of life—*we remembered*. It registered. Yes, we made it! We were all still drawing breath in our lungs. God had given us another week to live.

We said grace together and gave thanks for the food. Using a guide, we fumbled through our messy version of the Sabbath Dinner ceremony. Even though we didn't have the right bread, we passed it along. We didn't have the proper cups, but we filled them with our store-bought juice and clinked our glasses anyway. We passed the food, ate, and laughed.

It was not a regular dinner with friends. That dinner was a rhythm we had adopted together to anchor our hope in a world of despair. Together, we practiced the Jewish tradition of the Sabbath Dinner. While not expressly commanded in the Bible, it was a tradition the Israelites developed to position themselves for the day of rest to come, remembering and celebrating what God had done.

It might seem odd because none of us were culturally Jewish. None of us had ever done this before. We didn't really know what we were doing. I'm sure it was all wrong. But in the weeks leading up to this evening, everyone had been coming so exhausted, with heavy burdens and responsibilities on their shoulders. Collectively, we agreed we needed something to fight off the anxiety of a world in a downward spiral—a way to detach from it at the end of the week.

It was about that time when I heard from my friends at a church in Texas. Led by a Messianic Jew in their church, a group of them had started practicing the Sabbath Dinner together. They described it to me as a practice centered around remembering and celebrating who God is and what he has done. That sounded like something we could use.

When I suggested it to the group, everyone was eager to try it out and see what it might teach us. I Googled synagogues in the area and found a local rabbi who gave me some resources on practicing the Shabbat. Following their structure, we established the rhythm of practicing the Shabbat on Friday evening and kicked it off with the celebratory Sabbath Dinner.

What is the Sabbath Dinner?

> Sabbath (Shabbat) Dinner is a meal that starts the Christian day of rest, centered around remembering and celebrating what God has done.

The Sabbath Dinner is a powerful and liturgically rich meal that integrates storytelling, remembrance, and celebration in a powerful ceremony of rest. It is both simple to do and incredibly powerful. Every time we practice it, instead of stress and anxiousness, our hearts fill with joy and gratitude. In his book, *Created for Connection*, Rabbi Jason describes the ritual this way:

> Six days a week, we live under the tyranny of time as we exhaust ourselves in the pursuit of making a living and striving to fulfill our family and work commitments. But the Sabbath is different. On Sabbath, we rest from the daily grind and remember, celebrate, and experience the blessings of creation, the joy of relationships, and the freedom that comes with God's redemption through both the first redeemer Moses, and the second redeemer Messiah Yeshua (Jesus).[6]

This tradition provides a much-needed reprieve from the cycle of despair. How often do we not even notice or take time to celebrate when we accomplish a huge victory or our prayer has been answered? It's much easier to focus our attention on what's gone wrong rather than what's gone right. In this pattern, our soul withers.

Yet there is nearly always something worthy of celebration. The more attention we give it, our souls fill with hope. But to seek hope is to swim against the tide. That's why we need weekly rhythms that feed our soul the opposite of despair—*celebration*. Whether we practice the Sabbath Dinner in a large group, with a couple of people, with our partner, or with a roommate, it provides a key point in the week to help us focus on what God has done. It gives us fresh hope and strength.

The Power of Sabbath Dinner

1. Sabbath Dinner is an act of resistance against a godless worldview.

We must recognize that it is incredibly challenging to sit down and celebrate because we live in a world that does not. In his book *Sabbath as Resistance,* theologian Walter Brueggemann beautifully describes the challenge:

> In our own contemporary context of the rat race of anxiety, the celebration of Sabbath is an act of both resistance and alternative. It is resistance because it is a visible insistence that our lives are not defined by the production and consumption of commodity goods. Such an act of resistance requires enormous intentionality and communal reinforcement amid the barrage of seductive pressures from the insatiable insistences of the market, with its intrusion into every part of our life from the family to the national budget.[7]

How do we resist? Of course, the only way is to do something in the opposite spirit. If I hate a basketball team's success, then I resist by wearing their rivals' jerseys. In the same way, the Sabbath Dinner is an act of resistance against a tireless world.

When we gather around to eat our Sabbath meal, it is the practice of teaching our souls that we are not God. After all, we cannot take a break to celebrate if the world is resting on our shoulders. Celebration is the antithesis of this. We work hard, sow faithfully, and plant diligently, but in the end, we trust the results to God. And rest is the act of faith that exemplifies it. At rest, we reassign our responsibilities to God. It is the declaration that God holds the universe in his hands, not us.

2. The Sabbath Dinner reminds us of God's providence.

Gratitude is fast becoming a popular practice. It is because people realize that when we are future-obsessed, we forget what we already have. When we are hustling and bustling, we forget the clothes on their back, the food on our table, and the roof over our heads—all things we have already been provided.

Why is this? Work and remembrance are mutually exclusive. One cannot do both at the same time. Think about it: to work is to be future-thinking. It is to occupy our minds with what we don't have. Therefore, remembrance can only happen in rest. And that is the purpose of the Sabbath. It is so that we can remember.

By eating, we are doing so with the understanding that God has provided for this. God's providential hands have made every bite we take, every drink we sip, and every breath we draw possible. We can look back at our lives and realize that God is indeed watching over us. This remembrance strengthens and quiets our anxious souls and gives us courage.

In addition, a traditional Sabbath meal is rich in symbolism and biblical allusions. From the candles to the bread, each tells us a story from the Bible. Instead of being wrapped up in the anxious stories of the world, the Sabbath Dinner puts the providential story of God front and center of our lives.

3. The Sabbath Dinner restores strength to face the challenges ahead.

The Sabbath Dinner provides a collective release of anxiety for those who share it. Not only do we stop to remember what God has done for us, but we also hear the stories of what God has done for others. The gathering of these various stories from different sources affirms the belief that God is moving and cares for us. It's not all in our heads. God is good even when there is so much struggle. Together, we share this common story of God's providential hand.

> Work and remembrance are mutually exclusive. One cannot do both at the same time. Think about it: to work is to be future-thinking. It is to occupy our minds with what we don't have. Therefore, remembrance can only happen in rest. And that is the purpose of the Sabbath. It is so that we can remember.

We strengthen our horizontal bonds with one another, which supports us for what's ahead. And we strengthen our vertical bond with God, trusting more deeply that he will continue to provide for us.

How to Practice the Sabbath Dinner

If this is your first time celebrating the Sabbath Dinner as a family or small group, here is some guidance to help you. But first, a big disclaimer: the Shabbat Dinner has been practiced for hundreds of years by millions of Jewish people worldwide. I am not culturally Jewish. This guide is not an attempt at authenticity and does not describe what a Jewish house would do. Instead, see this as a quick introduction to my non-Jewish friends on participating in a spiritually rich tradition our faith friends have been practicing for centuries.

If you're interested in reading a more thorough, authentic guide, I encourage you to see Rabbi Jason Sobel's book, *Created for Connection*, as one great place to start.

Step 1: Invite friends and family to celebrate Shabbat.

The Sabbath dinner is a meal open to all. Families and friends gather around the table united by the common story of God and his goodness in our lives.

Typically, we celebrate with our life group from church, but we also invite others who are excited to celebrate the end of the week in a worshipful way. We understand everyone sitting around the table is unified not by blood, race, nationality, experience, or ideology but by being provided for as the children of God. It is a powerful reality.

Step 2: Set the table.

The table setting is more than chairs, tables, chicken, and potatoes. We do that every meal. No, this meal is special, like the meal after graduation or a wedding. There is a story to this meal. And people need to know the story.

We communicate the story first when we invite people. "Come over for Sabbath Dinner! It's a dinner to look back on the week and to remember and celebrate what God has done for us." But when family and guests are being seated, I usually give a small preamble to the story. It is usually centered around God's provision amidst chaos. It generally goes like this:

Welcome to Sabbath (or Shabbat) Dinner. It is a dinner to begin rest. It is a special dinner because we recognize that rest is not just rest. Rest is worship. We can celebrate, eat, and not work because we are celebrating that even when we rest, we serve a God who hung the universe, without needing anyone to work. We've come at the end of our busy weeks to enjoy each other's company, this good food, and to celebrate the goodness of God. It is worth celebrating because if you're breathing, you've made it!

You can use my little preamble or write your own.

Multi-sensory Elements

Typically in a traditional Shabbat Dinner, there are candles. The candles can signify the presence of God entering our homes. Feel free to use multi-sensory elements like this to convey richer storytelling.

Step 3: Giving and receiving of blessings.

The next step is the blessings. In Jewish tradition, the blessing centers around the roles of the family because of the biblical emphasis on the divine order and blessing of the family. There is a separate and formal blessing for the boys, girls, mothers, and then the fathers.

Usually, this is a formal blessing, but we have adapted it into a more casual blessing over the groups of people present. For example: "We bless you, mothers. We bless you with patience, courage, and grace. We bless you, boys. May God give you strength and humility as you get older."

Depending on the demographic makeup of your gathering, have a blessing for each group. You can adapt this any way you like.

To bless each other is to signify that we ourselves have been blessed. We are blessing out of an extension of the rich generosity of God, not ourselves.

Step 4: Break bread together.

Instead of worrying about the world, we are invited to recite the story of God. And in the story of God, we declare that no matter how chaotic the world is, we are not lost or abandoned. It is reciting the stories of God that refreshes our souls.

The way this story is communicated is through the symbol of bread—a powerful symbol in our faith. The unleavened bread symbolizes the Israelites running away from Egypt, while the bread that Jesus broke was his own body. In traditional Shabbat Dinners, challah bread is used to symbolize the escape from Egypt—a poignant story of how God miraculously delivered them into their land.

For your dinner, you may share a testimony of God's goodness you've experienced recently before breaking and sharing the bread around the table. As we eat, let us be reminded that the God of heaven watches over us.

This Meal Is Special

Consider eating something out of the ordinary for the meal. Even though we eat together for life group, when we celebrate Shabbat, I usually get meat from a butcher. It is a tad bit more expensive, but everyone looks forward to how delicious it is. However, it doesn't have to break the bank to be unique. The out-of-the-ordinary meal is simply to communicate, "This meal is special." Find a way to delight people, raise anticipation, and increase the celebration factor.

Step 5: Eat and share the story of God in our lives.

It is then we give thanks for the food and start eating. Having heard these rich stories of our faith, the table is filled with thanksgiving and wonder. Every bite is taken in gratitude and joy.

We talk casually and enjoy each other's company. Eventually, when the meal slows down, we will invite a more dedicated time of thanksgiving. To initiate this, we ask one to two questions for the group to share. "How did you see God at work this week? What are you thankful for this week?" These types of sharing have led to rich and worshipful conversations.

Step 6: Look ahead to the day of rest.

Once the meal is over and the guests have left, it is now the day of rest. That is a time to reflect on what rest looks like for you. Consider creating a list of things that are restful to your mind, body, and soul. Understanding what activities are restful requires a bit of forethought and exploration. Here are some on my list:

- being outside in nature
- having a light workout
- eating meals that restore my body
- doing things that keep my heart rate slow: driving slower, walking slower, getting up slower.

Part of the task of rest is creating a space where our souls are slow enough to talk to God.

If you're into calendaring, consider roughly charting out your rest days. Make it fun, restorative, and spiritually invigorating. Spend time reflecting and praying and getting good soul nourishment. Perhaps see a friend who gives you life. Whatever you do, try to make it a prayerful activity. Talk with God in the activity you are doing.

∽

As we go about our weeks, the Sabbath Dinner is a way to nurture and build upon the hope we've been given. The Sabbath Dinner allows us to remember and celebrate what God has done. This practice anchors our souls in hope, reminds us we are provided for, and strengthens us to face what's ahead.

Story Listening: Filtering the Headlines that Influence Our Hearts

"Notice the word 'hope' (in Psalm 62:5). The Hebrew term
literally means 'a cord, as an attachment.' Every one of
us is hanging on to something or someone for security.
... if it's someone or something other than God alone,
you're hanging on by a thread – the wrong thread."

BETH MOORE

Not too long ago, another national crisis was at play in our country. People from all sides were raging about their perspectives. In reading the endless stream of information, opinions, angsts, and worries, I noticed I began feeling depressed, discouraged, and anxious about the world we live in. Even though I then walked around running errands and getting groceries, the narrative followed me, with all its emotional turmoil. I wondered where God was in all of this.

Just as I was feeling like junk, a good Christian friend texted me. He is a missionary who lives halfway around the world. With exclamation marks all over the place, he messaged me frantically. I began wondering what was going on. I stopped reading the news for a moment and engaged with him in conversation.

He was in shock because of a miracle he had just experienced. A few weeks ago, through some unfortunate circumstances, he found out he was $18,000 in the hole for rent. (In the country he lives in, you need to pay for the entire year's rent at once.) He was in a bind and needed a miracle, and fast. Otherwise, they'd kick his whole family out.

With text bubbles firing quickly, he shared how the exact amount of money came in a day before the rent was due. He found an investment asset that was given to him that same week that was worth the exact amount of rent for the year. It was as if $18,000 popped out of thin air on his lap. He was elated with thanksgiving and praise. Some may have believed it was an amazing coincidence. But with it being the exact amount right when he needed it, my friend felt confident God had provided for him and his family, seemingly out of thin air.

My heart was in shock and my mood lifted. I thanked and praised God on his behalf. I wondered if I needed miracles too! Should I ask for my $18,000?

Even more so, I was shocked at what a juxtaposition I found myself in. Here in the midst of a national crisis, one of the most amazing provision stories came to pass. It made me think that perhaps God *is* always moving. In our crazy world, God is doing something. Maybe I'm just not listening to the right stories.

Why is it so depressing to read the news?

On any given week, it seems the American news cycle is churning away. It's either some massive political hit piece or some crisis we're dealing with or some animal is about to go extinct. It can really feel like the world is ending at any moment.

Since we transitioned from paid newspapers to online news reading, the entire nature of news reporting has changed. Instead of reporting boring information, news channels are beholden to paying advertisers. Advertisers only pay if people click on the ads, and people can only click on the ads if they visit the page. They'll only visit the page if the news article titles are catchy, scary, funny, provoking, or shocking—notice how I didn't say "true?"

To make money and remain solvent, major news outlets are no longer trying to get us to think; they're trying to get us to *feel*. They're trying to get us to feel angry, mad, upset, anxious, and scared. If we can feel those things, then we can click their pages, view their ads, and provide them with revenue.

We as consumers pay the true cost—the exhaustion of our souls. It can make us feel hopeless and tired. Many peers of mine who give themselves to the manifold stories of this world have become remarkably more depressed, disengaged, and less joyful. *Because the world is so hopeless, why should we do anything? Why should we move?* I certainly feel the temptation toward this mindset myself.

What do we do with the heaviness we feel from reading the news? What do we do with the endless barrage of bad news we face in our world today? This memory with my friend overseas led to the creation of a concept I call "Story Listening."

> Story Listening is the practice of filtering which stories shape our worldview and intentionally tuning into the stories of God.

I find that I need to start paying attention to the stories I listen to when several things happen:

- My hope meter is very low.
- I find myself annoyed or spiteful toward a person or group of people.

- I don't have a clear sense, passion, or purpose toward what God is doing around me.

To do this practice, I am not saying we should close our eyes, ears, and minds to all that is going on in the world. We are not to be ignorant of the woes of the world. But at the same time, we need to take stock of what's influencing our worldview. The practice of Story Listening is about stewarding the hope we have to offer in the world.

This practice is not new, just a new way of framing something that's been around for a long time. The concept reflects what Moses told the Israelites shortly after he gave them the laws of God. In Deuteronomy 6:8, he said, "You shall bind the commandments as a sign on your hand, and they shall be as frontlets between your eyes. You shall write them on the doorposts of your house and on your gates." Essentially, Moses was telling them to wear a Bible strapped to their foreheads, so that would be all they saw. A bit silly, but the imagery is provocative.

The heart of this exhortation is for the Israelites to always keep the stories of God at the center of their attention. The Israelites were to filter all other stories they took in through the lens of who God was and what he had done for them. It was a rhythm that was baked into the life of Israel. Hearing, listening, and meditating on the word of God would be central to their identity as a people as they lived among foreign nations. When they did so, it would form their thinking, value system, and expectations of what the world was about and where it was going.

The Power of Story Listening

1. Story Listening allows us to choose what stories are the loudest in our lives.

Too often, we take a passive role in which stories are shaping our lives. We take in the stories around us, and the loudest dominate our attention. These are the stories replaying on the news cycle or those everyone is sharing on social media. It isn't easy to binge-read the news, social media, or whatever news sources we follow and pretend that we can live out our lives full of hope and joy.

However, when we practice Story Listening, we begin to take ownership of the volume control. We have the power to turn the loudest stories down a few notches. We're not sticking our heads in the sand, but we're controlling how much command these stories have over us. Conversely, we can seek out stories that counterbalance all the bad news we hear—stories that remind us of God's power, presence, and faithfulness.

2. Story Listening exposes us to God's stories not published through the channels of the world.

What God is doing will hardly ever be reported on the news. A powerful family reconciliation, a sinner coming to repentance, a healing from cancer, miraculous generosity and provision—none of these get mass circulation. Yet they happen all around us, all the time! We cannot expect the channels of this world to publicize the stories of God—we must seek them out for ourselves.

As we seek out God's stories, we unsynchronize our sense of reality from the news cycle. We begin discovering stories of redemption, progress, healing, and beauty that reorient our concept of reality. That gives us a balanced lens to grieve the other stories without losing hope.

3. Story Listening teaches us how to live.

In the cycle of hopeless stories, we wonder what our place is in all this. It's easy to become angry and feel that our purpose is to rage on behalf of the tragedy. It's easy to take on a savior complex and believe that the solution to an incredibly complex problem sits heavily on our shoulders. It's also easy to feel crushed under the weight of it and become apathetic because we know we can never do enough to mend what ails our world.

Story Listening may not tell us exactly how to respond, but it gives us a greater sense of direction. Infusing us with fresh hope, Story Listening reminds us of the power of prayer. It reminds us of the power held in small acts of kindness or bravery. It reminds us that other people are out there and that it's not on our shoulders alone. Our hope in miracles slowly comes back to life.

To tune in is to recognize that, despite the loud noises of the world demanding our attention, we cannot solve every fire in the world. And not every battle on earth is meant to be taken up by us. Rather, my role in fixing and changing chaos depends on my ability to hear what God is doing and joining in it.

News/Social Media Fasts

Sometimes we need fixed periods where we withdraw from the public conversation to process, recenter, and regain clarity. If you feel this need, set aside a time when you fast from the news and/or social media. Try a day or even a week to start. Try deactivating your account or setting filters.

This works against the lie that we need to be constantly informed. While being informed gives us a momentary false sense of control, letting go of constant updates allows us to focus on what God's doing. Perhaps we can learn how to take in the news stream in a new way.

How to Practice Story Listening

Step 1: Audit and prune your information sources.

Take stock of the news stories and social media personalities you follow. None of these may be necessarily *wrong*. However, they may not be helping the state of your soul at the moment. The Apostle Paul said, "Everything is permissible, but not everything is beneficial." (1 Corinthians 10:23) Are all our sources of information benefiting our soul?

To evaluate this, ask:

- What kind of world is portrayed?
- What emotions are they trying to strike with their audience?
- According to them, who is the enemy?
- Are all my sources creating an echo chamber?
- What do I feel about God and others when I take in this info?

Perhaps listening to these sources makes it harder for me to be merciful, loving, patient, and hopeful. Maybe a certain source is narrowing my vision too much. Sometimes I need the maturity to recognize certain news stations, public personalities, and types of conversations are not helping me.

If you find this is the case, change channels, unfollow accounts, unsubscribe to newsletters—whatever you feel God is convicting you to prune so you can bear the fruits of the spirit more readily.

Seeking Neutral Sources

If you're exhausted from emotionally draining news sources like I am, consider finding alternative news sources. I subscribe to a few newsletters that have simple bullet-point lists of what's happening in the world. They have helped me stay in tune with what's going on without the drama of someone click-baiting me.

Note: I would like to give examples here, but the digital space moves so much quicker than a print book, so I recognize if I list them here, they may not even exist by the time you read this. I'd still love to share examples with you through my website and social media which I can keep up to date long after this book comes out.

Step 2: Seek out stories in the community of God.

We need to feed our hearts with the stories of God in our faith communities. I often find that people experience God regularly, but we don't always share or hear about it.

At the small group I lead, I regularly ask, "What is God doing in your lives?" We go around the room and we share stories. Those have proven rich and powerful times. Often, we see themes of God working in similar ways among different people.

Ask this question to someone in your community. Take someone out to coffee and say, "What is God doing in your life?" Let the stories fill your heart with hope. Consider approaching one of your church leaders and saying, "I'd love to hear what God is doing in our church so that I can pray and participate as well."

Suppose you don't have someone around you who you can ask in the moment. In that case, there are an enormous number of amazing testimonies online. Sometimes I will turn on YouTube testimonies or sermons while I'm doing household chores. It is great to hear what God is doing in the larger body.

Step 3: Remember God stories in your own life.

Lastly, we need to remember the stories of God already happening in our lives. I forget what he is doing in my own life in the busyness and craziness of chaos. And because of that, I feel lost.

Yet it is so encouraging to reflect on the stories of encouragement, healing, redemption, and triumph God has already woven into our stories. It is powerful to reflect on the prayers he has already answered as fuel for our hope as we wait for the things to come.

In particular, think back on where you were one year ago today. What prayers has God answered since then? What testimonies have you seen come to pass? In what ways has God grown you? From there, you can further consider what prayers God has answered in the last several years and in your life.

Revisit Old Journals

Many times, we don't see what God is doing in our lives simply because we don't remember. If only there was a place where we could actively see the things we reflected on in our lives. *That's right, our journals!* I make it a practice to dig up and read my old journals. It's like reading a time capsule. More importantly, it's edifying to read the things I prayed for. Many times, I will marvel because only in rereading do I realize: "Wow, God really answered my prayers."

In addition, I am thrilled because I begin seeing the larger thread of what God is doing in my life. Typically, we only see life daily, but reading old journals allows us to see the more significant movement of God over a season. There are seasons where extended challenges and struggles have yielded specific growth points in me. And those seasons have also allowed me to see the sovereign hand of God. Once I see how he has moved in the past, I can comprehend what he is doing in the present and align myself with it.

One way we steward our hearts is by taking control of the stories we hear and what space they take up in our hearts. In chaos, there are so many troublesome and hopeless stories. Story Listening is the practice of turning down the volume on stories that deter me from God's story and tuning into the stories that help me live faithfully.

The Enemy Blessing:
Growing Love in a Hostile World

No one heals himself by wounding another.

AMBROSE, 4TH CENTURY

We may not be able to prevent other people from being our enemies, but we can prevent ourselves from being enemies toward others.

WARREN WIERSBE

In one season, I began to dislike a specific person in my life. For months, I had been complaining to my wife about this person. Our values could not have been more different. We thought differently about faith, life, politics—everything.

That would have been fine—agree to disagree—if not for the fact that this person was in a leadership position over my life, and their decisions started to affect me. Every decision they made seemed to be a slap in the face of what I believed. *They were so annoying!* I constantly ruminated.

Every time I saw this person, I tried my best to avoid them. But I couldn't. Because the saddest part—bear with me here—was that this person went to the same church as I did. Worshiping the same God. Loving the same people.

One morning as I spent time with God, I felt a nudge from the Lord—*pay attention to those.* The words, "Pray for your enemies" from Matthew 5:44 came to mind. I felt the Lord challenge me to begin praying for this person.

I was a bit taken aback at first. "Enemy" is a harsh word. When I think of enemies, I often think of soldiers on opposite sides of battle lines, politicians vying for the same seat, or Batman against the Joker. This person wasn't my *enemy*, I reasoned. They were just actively opposing all my goals and values while I oozed secret hostility toward them. "Okay, I guess I see it now," I told God. I guess they were my enemy. This clarification was unfortunate because this now placed them squarely into the category of people God commanded me to bless.

"All right," I said begrudgingly. "Because you said so, I will do it."

I closed my eyes and prayed the simplest prayer I could pray.

"Lord, bless this person. I know you love them."

Every word was hard to come by because of the bitterness in my heart.

Yet as I prayed, an image materialized in my mind. It was a picture of Jesus, and he was in heaven looking down on the person I was praying for.

Jesus' face was what shocked me because his face was unlike my own. I grumble, moan, and grit my teeth when I think about this person. But when I saw Jesus's face, I saw his loving gaze. I saw that he truly loved them. Not in the grit-your-teeth kind of way. He genuinely enjoyed and was delighted with this person. His smile was the most genuine smile I had ever seen. I almost teared up because of his heart overflowing for them.

Seeing this image melted something cold and judgmental in me. Watching Jesus's loving face, I became aware of the absence of that love in my heart. I knew I was wrong.

I had never understood the power of blessing my enemy until this moment. While it wasn't all easy from there on, I did learn that heaven's perspective of my enemies is different than my own, and I can tap into that perspective to soften the hardness of my heart.

In times of peace, there may be people who annoy us or those we disagree with, but the idea of them being enemies is further from our minds. Yet chaos is a force that polarizes us. When there is public chaos, enemy lines suddenly seem much more apparent. There is nothing like looking at public commentary after a major national crisis. Due to the rapid news cycle and social media, the world we live in has turned American discourse into a shouting match. If you have never read the comments section on any news article—trust me, you're not missing out—people are shouting at each other, name-calling, and swearing. They are angry. Even though they don't know the other person on the internet, they think they know everything about them. They feel entitled and empowered to tear that person down.

Where does our rage for our enemy originate? Why do we have images and visages of people we disregard and push aside? Why are we so quick to make enemies of the people that stand on the other side? These are questions that I must ask myself because the more chaotic things are, the more tempted I am to make enemies of people I don't know. But why?

The answer to this question is in the words of Jesus. Jesus was onto something when he said in Matthew 7:3, "Why do you look at the speck of sawdust in your brother's eye and pay no attention to the plank in your own eye?" In this teaching, he reveals something critical: when we look at someone with judgment, it says more about the state of our heart than theirs. In other words, the problem isn't my enemy. Perhaps the problem is me. The rage toward my enemy is simply my own bitterness, bias, and insecurity lashing outward to find a target.

You've likely heard the verse about praying for our enemies before. But I don't know hardly anyone who has lived out The Enemy Blessing as a regular spiritual discipline.

> The Enemy Blessing is the practice of adopting God's perspective toward those in opposition to us.

While "blessing" has many meanings, the core of The Enemy Blessing is to pray for their wellbeing. This may mean praying for their goals and dreams to come to pass. It may mean praying for the health of their family. Perhaps it means considering the needs of their heart in this season and asking God to fill them. Maybe it means praying they get the job they want. This can be trying, as it goes against what we may naturally wish for someone who irritates, opposes, or even persecutes us.

To embrace this practice, we must confront the ugliness and hypocrisy in our hearts. It's countercultural, sometimes taboo, and very vulnerable. Likely for these reasons, few people model this practice. Yet without seeing this humility and transparency, we lack a model to follow. Meanwhile, as we are living in increasingly hostile environments, it is easy for our hearts to become filled with hate, malice, and vengeance. This is why The Enemy Blessing is so important.

Blessing Enemies Is Not Permitting Abuse

If we think of someone as an enemy or need to forgive them, it may be because they have harmed us somehow. This can happen over the natural course of a relationship, with no malicious intent. However, some forms of harm are more severe and qualify as abuse. Abuse can appear in a number of forms—physical, mental, emotional, spiritual, and sexual.

I want to clarify that this chapter on forgiving our enemies, does not mean allowing people who have abused us to continue doing so or to reenter our lives and abuse us again. The Enemy Blessing is simply a practice that, over time, works to remove the bitterness so it does not keep a stronghold over our hearts. It is not a statement about what that relationship should look like in the future.

Forgiving and praying for someone does not necessarily mean letting them back into your life. As part of this process, you may eventually let someone back into your life with certain boundaries in place so they cannot continue harming you. In other instances, you can forgive someone but discontinue your relationship with them. That is not at all antithetical to blessing our enemies. If you have a relationship like that, I recommend reaching out to trusted community to help you determine what that relationship should look like going forward.

The Power of the Enemy Blessing

We go into praying for our enemies with the limitations of our humanness—our selfishness, hatred, and pain. But we come out of praying for our enemies a different person. How does it accomplish this?

1. Blessing our enemies reveals the limits of our hearts.

Trying to bless our enemies is like God handing us a gift to give to someone else. But instead of giving it to them, you clench your fist and hang onto the gift with all your might. *They don't deserve it! They shouldn't be blessed!* At that moment, we must reckon with why we are holding on so tightly. For in understanding our hesitation, the blockages in our hearts become revealed.

When I pray for people I do not like, I must confront why I do not like them. And most of the time, they are my own reasons. It may be because of a bias of judgment I hold. Sometimes it's because they have something I wish I had. More than not, it's because I am in pain, have unforgiveness, am jealous, or feel threatened. We are convinced we need them to lose or be proven wrong for us to resolve these issues and set them at peace, but that is false. The problem we need to fix is between ourselves and God. Our enemies serve as a mirror to see ourselves more clearly and where we need to grow.

2. Blessing our enemies leads us to see people through God's eyes.

Our eyes are informed by our sin, selfishness, wounds, history, assumptions, and limited understanding. However, God has a perspective of people that is not clouded by any of those things. From this perspective, he commands that we ask for a blessing on their lives.

Praying for people is to see people from God's heart. When we see people from the vantage of God, we see people for who they are. We see people past the pain and grievance they've caused us. We see them as people made in God's image and whom he loves deeply. In doing so, we allow our enemies to become a force that shapes us further into the likeness of Christ.

3. Blessing our enemies creates supernatural unity amid the world's polarization.

Our world is constantly moving toward tribalization, dividing people into ideas, lifestyles, political parties, experiences, etc. Headlines are tailored to create "us" and "them" categories, even and especially within the Church body. As a result, the Church mirrors the fractured nature of our world when we are to be set apart.

Christ's love is the only antidote to all the hatred and vitriol. It is not my patience, love, or kindness. It is God's love in me that is unfathomable, illogical, and completely beautiful. To pray for our enemies is to open the valve of our hearts to God's love. It is to relinquish the small size of our hearts and to wish for blessing.

When we get filled, our hearts become impervious to the world's tactics that try to polarize and separate us. With no gaping holes for offense, jadedness, or bitterness, the rumors and headlines have no place to reside. Instead, our unity becomes a testimony to God's love—a love foreign to the world. We cannot achieve it without his intervention.

How to Practice The Enemy Blessing

Step 1: Identify your enemies.

As I mentioned earlier, we don't always think of people as our enemies by default. But take a moment to evaluate:

- Who in your life do you feel actively opposes your values or goals?
- Is there anyone hostile toward you?
- Who do you often feel irritation toward?
- Who feels like they're on the opposite team?
- Is there someone who makes you want to leave the room when they enter?

- Is there anyone who has wounded you, and you still feel bitterness toward them?

It may be someone who has been an enemy of ours for a long time, or perhaps it's someone who became our enemy just this week. It could be a stranger, someone at work, at church, or someone we love very much but butt heads with.

Reflect and ask yourself: who have I made into an enemy?

Start Simple

It is *hard* to pray for enemies. Maybe at one point in our lives, we'll pray great blessings for them. But we're not there yet, and it's okay.

Whenever we're newbies at something, whether it's playing a sport, learning to run, or lifting weights, the adage is true: start small.

Start with simple prayers:

"Lord, bless them."

"Help them."

"Thank you for their life."

These prayers do not have to be impassioned or eloquent. Start with prayers a three-year-old would say. You will find that as you start small, your heart will begin to open.

Step 2: Ask God what this enemy shows me about my own heart.

The people I resent, am annoyed with, dislike, and hate often reflect the unmet needs, untended wounds, or unchecked biases of my heart. Divert attention away from their actions or characteristics and focus on you. What does this enemy represent to you? What are they blocking from your life? If they are standing in the way of your peace, for example, ask Jesus for that peace instead of predicating it on your enemy's failure. The key to freedom is not focusing on others but on the state of our hearts.

Step 3: Ask for God's perspective of this person.

Start by asking God for his picture of this person in your mind. What does he see? What strengths does he notice? What does he appreciate about them?

Next, ask God what he *feels* about this person. Is it affection, protectiveness, trust, patience, gentleness, understanding, etc.? Ask him to help you experience even just a bit of what he feels for them.

Step 4: Pray for forgiveness for your enemies.

Reconciliation requires two parties, but forgiveness only requires one. Forgiveness is something we do on our own. Unforgiveness is like drinking poison and wishing your enemy drank it. Speaking forgiveness over our enemies for any way they have slighted us is the path to removing the poison from our hearts.

Pray a prayer of forgiveness between you and the Lord. "Lord, I forgive this person for what they have done to me. Whether they intended or not, I release them from the debt owed to me by their wrongdoing, and I bless them in Jesus's name."

The decision to pray this prayer does not necessarily mean our emotions toward them have changed. However, this decision to forgive, repeated in lieu of grumbling, brings our minds and emotions into alignment with this action over time.

 ✑

The Enemy Blessing is critical when more and more people are becoming hostile and polarized. When things get more chaotic, we need this practice to center our hearts on the love of Christ and to root out the things which breed hate, anger, and resentment toward the world we love.

One-Second Prayers: Our Lifeline in the Heat of the Moment

Is prayer your steering wheel or your spare tire?
CORRIE TEN BOOM

If the heart wanders or is distracted, bring it back to the point quite gently and replace it tenderly in its Master's presence. And even if you did nothing during the whole of your hour but bring your heart back and place it again in our Lord's presence, though it went away every time you brought it back, your hour will be very well employed.
ST. FRANCIS DE SALES

"Phil, we need you for a moment."
I quickly stopped what I was doing. I got pulled into an emergency meeting. Once the door closed behind us, my colleagues began discussing an issue with a teammate at work. The person had

done something that went against company policy and now the team was looking to me for a quick answer on how to proceed.

Unfortunately, they caught me by surprise. Usually, as prepared as I am, I spend time thinking about conversations before they happen. I plan my day and think about the conversations I need to have, what angle I'll approach them from, what I will say, and what I will not say. But not this time. It came as a big surprise, and I had no idea what to say.

A Bible verse from Matthew 10 flashed into my mind. "Don't worry about what you will say or how you will say it. At that time you will be given the right words to say." *Okay Phil, when you don't know what to say, ask God for the words.*

In my mind, I asked God: *Help me Holy Spirit. Help me to know what to say.* All I could do in that moment was listen to my teammates with one ear and listen to see if the Holy Spirit had anything to say with the other.

Out of nowhere, an idea came to mind. It sounded wise, and it did not seem to originate from me. I rolled with it.

I suggested this action to my coworkers. They stood for a few moments and listened. To my surprise, they all agree this was the right course of action.

Phew! Where did that idea come from?

What do we do when we don't have time to pray?

I love my set-aside times with God, but we can't spend every waking moment in the prayer closet. Sometimes when we encounter a situation out and about in the world, we literally don't have time to pray. Sometimes we're in back-to-back meetings for multiple hours straight. What do we do then?

The answer is what I call One-Second Prayers. One-Second Prayers are something absolutely everybody has time to do. Sure, you may be busy. But *everyone* has one second to spare.

> One-Second Prayers are short one-sentence prayers we pray in
> the moment to connect us with God and ask for help.

The inspiration for the One-Second Prayer is from the life of Nehemiah. Nehemiah was a prophet who was a cupbearer to the King. He desperately wanted to see his home country, Israel, rebuilt. One day, he gets a moment with the King. Noticing Nehemiah's face, the King asks, "Why are you sad?" Nehemiah has a rare opportunity with this influential man, and he takes advantage of it. The text goes as follows:

> Then the king said to me, "What are you requesting?" So I prayed to the God of heaven. And I said to the king, "If it pleases the king, and if your servant has found favor in your sight, that you send me to Judah, to the city of my fathers' graves, that I may rebuild it.

In verse 4, the King asks Nehemiah a question in his presence. And then it says that Nehemiah prayed. And then the very next verse, he comes up with the answer to the King's question. Nehemiah optimizes his moment with the King in order to benefit his people. It seemed to be a well-thought-out response in a high-stakes situation, but this entire exchange happened over a few seconds. Nehemiah certainly didn't have time to go somewhere and pray for a long time after the King asked him the question.

I think Nehemiah prayed a One-Second Prayer. In that short moment between sentences, he uttered a short prayer under his breath. It was not long, nor poetic, but it was genuine and real. And God answered.

A lot of us find ourselves in Nehemiah's position. We're in the in-between. A moment of pressure. A split-second decision and we need God's help. We need God's blessing. If that's the case, and we don't have a lot of time. Try the One-Second Prayer.

The Power of One-Second Prayers

1. One-Second Prayers are timely and authentic.

Sometimes, we meet with God as if a guest is coming to our home. We empty the sink of dishes and dust all the little corners no one would ever notice. In other words, we sometimes need to be prepared and put together to be in God's presence.

While there's a benefit to this in wanting to treat God as an honored guest, we don't need to primp and prepare to be with our best friend. With our best friends, we utter what's on our minds without worrying about polishing it. Rather than a sign of disrespect, it is a sign of intimacy and the easiness of being with someone you love and who loves you. One-Second Prayers invite us into this kind of organic relationship where we can call out to God in the moment, even if it's messy.

One of the things I do to practice this relationship dynamic is imagine Jesus being with me in whatever I am doing, and then talking to him. If I'm driving, I imagine Jesus is sitting in the passenger seat. If I'm in a meeting at work, I'll imagine Jesus took the empty chair in the meeting. That helps me contextually talk to him. I talk to him like he's there with me, and I speak to him about the things going on in my life.

You don't need a long time to do this kind of prayer. Just imagine Jesus being with you wherever you are and say a One-Second Prayer like a friend talking to another friend.

2. One-Second Prayers recenter prayer on the connection over length or eloquence.

Longer prayers are not necessarily more powerful. In fact, Jesus complained about the Pharisees giving long prayers. They did it for attention. That's not to say that every long prayer is inauthentic or disingenuous. But it does show that length and authenticity are not the same, and Jesus values the latter.

As long as our prayer is genuine, it's a prayer that's heard. One-Second Prayers act on that truth.

3. One-Second Prayer makes the ever-presence of God more tangible in our lives.

Because One-Second Prayers don't require any particular place, posture, or preparation, they have the ability to permeate every moment and sphere of our lives. Whether we're in a meeting, in the shower, talking to our kids, on the phone with a parent, in line at the grocery store, or in a job interview, there is no place we ever go where we could not pray a One-Second Prayer. God hears us wherever we go.

God is delighted when we seek him out in every moment like this rather than waiting for a set time or place. As a matter of fact, I think this is what the Bible means when the writer of Hebrews said Jesus was constantly in prayer. Yes, he went off to the mountainsides for formal times of prayer with his disciples. Still, the rest of the time, the majority of his days, I bet, were filled with a long string of One-Second Prayers. As a result, Jesus was engaged with his Father every moment.

How to Practice One-Second Prayers

Step 1: Build a repertoire of One-Second Prayers.

If you're going to pray One-Second Prayers, I find it helpful to build an arsenal of prayers to whip out in any given situation. These are prayers I know to pray, whether I'm about to have an important meeting, someone asks me a surprising question, or I run into a situation where I have absolutely no idea what to do.

Here are my favorites:
- "Help me, Holy Spirit."
- "Lord, give me strength."
- "Jesus, show me where you are."

- "Help me to be patient, God."

What are One-Second Prayers can you imagine yourself using in the heat of the moment?

Step 2: Identify times of your day when you want to pray One-Second Prayers.

Think about a typical day. Where are the points of stress you usually encounter? What are the moments you find yourself losing—or almost losing—your cool? Perhaps it's when your spouse does that one thing that annoys you, when you open your email in the morning, when you get that call from your child's teacher, when the essay you worked on for hours suddenly gets deleted, or when you just realized you've been scrolling for an hour and need some motivation to move on. What moments in your day do you want to begin inviting Jesus in through One-Second Prayers?

Step 3: Pray.

The last step is so simple because this practice is so simple. Use those One-Second Prayers you've been saving for this moment. Whisper them under your breath, write them on a sticky note, jot them down in your phone notepad, or just pray them silently in your head.

When it comes down to it, this practice is about training ourselves to reach out to God in our daily lives. Doing this teaches us to abide in him and let him permeate our days.

Not everyone has time to do long prayers in the heat of a moment. One-Second Prayers are a great way to connect with God amid a chaotic day. Their brevity doesn't make them any less effective. Rather, they invite God's divine involvement no matter how crazy our days get.

Afterword

We know by now that chaos is not an if but a when. We must be people of God who understand the times we live in and know how to thrive in the midst of it all. Yet we are fully capable of establishing rhythms in our life that move us from surviving to thriving as we were created to.

Faith practices are necessary for any Christian who seeks to establish these chaos-proof rhythms. We've explored fifteen spiritual practices that serve every Christian as the distress of our lives increases. We looked at the importance of leaving our contexts regularly to position ourselves for transformation. Then we looked at practices that call for stillness so that we can gain clarity. Next, we looked at the practices that confront our wounds and bring healing. Lastly, we looked at the practices that help us to steward our transformation and become forces of peace in our world.

In these practices, we recognize our weaknesses and position ourselves before God in life-transforming ways. And as we do so, the roots in our lives become so deep that no amount of wind can push us around. Over time, we develop immense spiritual resilience that allows us to partake in God's dreams.

I pray these practices will be like a tool belt for you in times of need and that the Holy Spirit will show you when and where to use them. I pray you will have the courage to give yourselves to God in these ways. I pray this book helps you grow into the resilience and calling God has for you.

Notes

1   "Boost Your Mental Health by Spending Time Outside," Harvard T.H. Chan School of Public Health, last modified June 24, 2022, accessed August 5, 2022, https://www.hsph.harvard.edu/news/hsph-in-the-news/boost-your-mental-health-by-spending-time-outside/

2   Daniel Levitin, *The Organized Mind: Thinking Straight in the Age of Information Overload*, (New York City: Dutton, 2015), 33.

3   Kevin McSpadden, "Science: You Now Have a Shorter Attention Span Than a Goldfish," Time, last modified May 14, 2015, accessed August 12, 2022, https://time.com/3858309/attention-spans-goldfish/.

4   "Turkish Sheep Die in 'Mass Jump,'" BBC News, last modified July 8, 2005, accessed November 18, 2022, http://news.bbc.co.uk/2/hi/europe/4665511.stm.

5   Ryan Faughnder, "2020 Global Streaming Subscriptions Top 1 Billion amid COVID," Los Angeles Times, last modified March 18, 2021, accessed August 2, 2022, https://www.latimes.com/entertainment-arts/business/story/2021-03-18/streaming-milestone-global-subscriptions-passed-1-billion-last-year-mpa-theme-report.

6   Jason Sobel, *Created for Connection: A Sabbath Supper Club Guide*, (Valley Village: Fusion Global, 2021).

7   Walter Bruggeman, *Sabbath as Resistance: Saying No to the Culture of Now*, (Louisville: Westminster John Knox Press, 2017).

Bibliography

"Boost Your Mental Health by Spending Time Outside." Harvard T.H. Chan School of Public Health. Last modified June 24, 2022, accessed August 5, 2022. https://www.hsph.harvard.edu/news/hsph-in-the-news/boost-your-mental-health-by-spending-time-outside/.

Bruggeman, Walter. *Sabbath as Resistance: Saying No to the Culture of Now.* Louisville: Westminster John Knox Press, 2017.

Faughnder, Ryan. "2020 Global Streaming Subscriptions Top 1 Billion amid COVID." Los Angeles Times. Last modified March 18, 2021, accessed August 2, 2022. https://www.latimes.com/entertainment-arts/business/story/2021-03-18/streaming-milestone-global-subscriptions-passed-1-billion-last-year-mpa-theme-report.

Levitin, Daniel. *The Organized Mind: Thinking Straight in the Age of Information Overload.* New York City: Dutton, 2015).

McSpadden Kevin. "Science: You Now Have a Shorter Attention Span Than a Goldfish," Time. Last modified May 14, 2015, accessed August 12, 2022. https://time.com/3858309/attention-spans-goldfish/.

Sobel, Jason. *Created for Connection: A Sabbath Supper Club Guide.* Valley Village: Fusion Global, 2021.

"Turkish Sheep Die in 'Mass Jump.'" BBC News. Last modified July 8, 2005, accessed November 18, 2022. http://news.bbc.co.uk/2/hi/europe/4665511.stm.

About the Author

Phil Chan is a blogger turned author passionate about seeing Christians thrive in today's world. He graduated with a Master of Divinity degree from Fuller Theological Seminary and has been writing for over twenty years from phillipchan.org.

Phil's shorter works include a guide called *Journaling for Spiritual Transformation* and another piece called *God Moments* to help busy people continually experience God's presence. More recently, he has taught spiritual practices and habits to help people develop resilience and realize their full potential in God.

Beyond writing and teaching, Phil is an avid technologist, organizational leader, squatter of heavy weights, wrangler of multiple young kids, lover of his wife, home chef of kid-approved meals, and leader at church in various positions.

He resides in Pasadena, California where he enjoys the weather and local taco trucks with his wife and four kids.

To learn more and connect with Phil, visit phillipchan.org.

Note from the Publisher

We at Berry Powell Press publish books that meet specific requirements of quality and message. *Rhythms of Resilience* by Phil Chan fully embodies our values and mission, and we are proud to offer this important book to our readers.

Spiritual practices are at the heart of most, if not all, spiritual traditions. This is certainly true of those rooted in the long history of Judeo-Christian thought. Its many subgroups have developed Christian spiritual practices to serve a variety of purposes. *Rhythms of Resilience* joins this longstanding conversation by pin-pointing the need for today's believer to successfully cope with the enormous pressures of a globalized and interconnected world. While history reveals other times of acute stress, what we face today is unprecedented.

Not all spiritual practices are beneficial in dealing with stress, crisis, and a sense of overwhelm. Phil's path to stabilizing hearts and minds through practical ways works to maintain and strengthen a believer's connection with God—the source of peace that defies human abilities.

Because we at BPP provide in-depth mentoring services, we get to know our authors well. Our relationship with Phil has given us confidence in his integrity to live true to his message. Phil walks the talk, having confronted many challenges using these steps. Phil, his family, and those who have studied and applied these spiritual practices have substantiated their effectiveness and sound wisdom.

The Berry Powell Press staff cultivates authors and their life-changing messages through a collaborative community of authors and publishing professionals. If you have a message that needs to become a book, please visit our website at www.berrypowellpress.com.

Berry Powell Press is a hybrid publishing house that publishes authors with transformational perspectives on timely personal and societal challenges. We provide our authors with in-depth mentorship and collaborative assistance to create life-changing books. Additionally, we assist them in building book-based businesses that can impact the largest audience possible. We publish fiction and non-fiction for adults and children.

Made in the USA
Monee, IL
02 January 2023

24151727R00127